D1706875

Mediterranean
Diet Cookbook for Beginners

1200+

Easy and Flavorful Recipes,

30-Day Meal Plan to Help You Build Healthy Habits

Maureen Hussey

Contents

Poultry And Meats 15

Fish And Seafood 27

Vegetable Mains And Meatless

Sides , Salads, And Soups 53

Beans , Grains, And Pastas 65

Fruits, Desserts And Snacks 79

Introduction

I was born in Patras, Greece, when my family moved there before I was born. Due to the unique Mediterranean climate, which is perfect for growing fruits and vegetables, various fruits and vegetables have also become an important part of the Greek diet, so I grew up cooking and eating Mediterranean food.

The Mediterranean diet isn't just a diet - it's a lifestyle. Originally formulated in the 1960s, it drew on Greek, Italian, French and Spanish cuisines. In the decades since, it has also incorporated other Mediterranean cuisines such as those from the Balkans, the Middle East, North Africa and Portugal. While tasty plant protein, tasty fish, occasional red meat, and plenty of fresh fruits and vegetables are the hallmarks of a diet, you can also enjoy grains, or even a glass of red wine, while getting major health benefits. The Mediterranean diet has been shown to be effective for weight loss, it may even prevent disease and increase your life expectancy.

This cookbook is about the most popular Mediterranean diet recommendations for 2022. See Mediterranean Food Recipes for foods from the surrounding Mediterranean region that maximize your body's sources of vitamins, minerals, and other micronutrients. Overall, food combinations in a healthy lifestyle are associated with improved health.

I look forward to this Mediterranean diet cookbook guiding you to better understand the Mediterranean diet and embarking on this exciting journey with you to achieve a holistic health makeover.

What is the Mediterranean Diet?

The Mediterranean diet or way of eating is a plant-heavy diet that focuses more on vegetables, fruits, whole grains, beans, nuts and legumes, as well as some lean proteins from fish and poultry, and good fats from things like extra virgin olive oil. As you see at the very top of the Mediterranean diet pyramid are red meats and sweets which are enjoyed less frequently.

The Mediterranean diet originates in the food cultures of ancient civilizations which developed around the Mediterranean Basin and is based on the regular consumption of olive oil (as the main source of added fat), plant foods (cereals, fruits, vegetables, legumes, tree nuts, and seeds), the moderate consumption of fish, seafood, and dairy, and low-to-moderate alcohol (mostly red wine) intake, balanced by a comparatively limited use of red meat and other meat products.

Traditional eating habits seen in geographical territories surrounding the Mediterranean Sea, although differentiated by some food choices and cooking practices specific to each country and culture, share a common set of basic features :emphasizes vegetables, fruits, whole grains, beans and legumes; includes low-fat or fat-free dairy products, fish, poultry, non-tropical vegetable oils and nuts; and limits added sugars, sugary drinks, sodium, highly processed foods, refined carbohydrates, saturated fats, and fatty or processed meats.

This diet can play an important role in preventing heart disease and stroke and in reducing risk factors such as obesity, diabetes, high cholesterol and high blood pressure. There is some evidence that a Mediterranean diet rich in virgin olive oil may help your body remove excess cholesterol from your arteries and keep your blood vessels open, helping you achieve the American Heart Association's recommendations for a healthy dietary pattern.

The Mediterranean Diet Pyramid

Scientific research has shown that the benefits brought by Mediterranean-derived dietary interventions not only in the primary and secondary prevention of cardiovascular disease, but also in the therapeutic approach of obesity, type 2 diabetes, metabolic syndrome, cancer or neurodegenerative diseases.

MEDITERRANEAN DIET

8 Easy Ways to Follow the Mediterranean Diet for Better Health

Cook with Olive Oil

If you've been cooking with vegetable oil or coconut oil, make the switch to extra-virgin olive oil. Olive oil is rich in monounsaturated fatty acids, which may improve HDL cholesterol, the "good" type of cholesterol. Use olive oil in homemade salad dressings and vinaigrettes. Drizzle it on finished dishes like fish or chicken to boost flavor. Swap olive oil for butter in mashed potatoes, pasta and more.

Eat More Fish

The go-to protein in the Mediterranean diet is fish. In particular, this diet emphasizes fatty fish like salmon, sardines and mackerel. These fish are rich in heart- and brain-healthy omega-3 fatty acids. Even those fish that are leaner and have less fat (like cod or tilapia) are still worth it, as they provide a good source of protein. Cooking fish in parchment paper or foil packets is one no-fuss, no-mess way to put dinner on the table. Or try incorporating it in some of your favorite foods, like tacos, stir-fries and soups.

Eat Veggies All Day Long

Featured Recipe: Baked Vegetable Soup

If you look at your diet and worry that there's barely a green to be seen, this is the perfect opportunity to fit in more veggies. A good way to do this is to eat one serving at snack time, like crunching on bell pepper strips or throwing a handful of spinach into a smoothie, and one at dinner, like these quick and easy side dishes. Aim for at least two servings per day. More is better. At least three servings can help you bust stress, Australian research notes.

Help Yourself to Whole Grains

Featured Recipe: Italian Tarragon Buckwheat

Experiment with "real" whole grains that are still in their "whole" form and haven't been refined. Quinoa cooks up in just 20 minutes, making it a great side dish for week-night meals. Barley is full of fiber and it's filling: pair it with mushrooms for a steamy, satisfying soup. A hot bowl of oatmeal is perfect for breakfast on a cold winter morning.

Snack on Nuts

Featured Recipe: Garlic-yogurt Dip With Walnuts

Nuts are another Mediterranean diet staple. Grabbing a handful, whether that's almonds, cashews or pistachios, can make for a satisfying, on-the-go snack. One study in Nutrition Journal found that if people replaced their standard snack (cookies, chips, crackers, snack mix, cereal bars) with almonds, their diets would be lower in empty calories, added sugar and sodium. Plus, nuts contain more fiber and minerals, such as potassium, than processed snack foods.

Enjoy Fruit for Dessert

Generally a good source of fiber, vitamin C and antioxidants, fresh fruit is a healthy way to indulge your sweet tooth. If it helps you to eat more, add a little sugar-drizzle slices of pear with honey or sprinkle a little brown sugar on grapefruit. Keep fresh fruit visible at home and keep a piece or two at work so you have a healthful snack when your stomach starts growling.

Sip (a Little) Wine

The people who live along the Mediterranean-the Spanish, Italian, French, Greek and others-are not known to shy away from wine, but that doesn't mean you should pour it at your leisure. Dietitians and experts who developed the Mediterranean diet for the New England Journal of Medicine study advised women to stick to a 3-ounce serving, and men to a 5-ounce serving, per day. When you do sip, try to do so with a meal-even better if that meal is shared with loved ones.

Savor Every Bite

Featured Recipe: Bell Pepper & Chickpea Salad

Eating like a Mediterranean is as much lifestyle as it is diet. Instead of gobbling your meal in front of the TV, slow down and sit down at the table with your family and friends to savor what you're eating. You're more apt to eat just until you're satisfied than until you're busting-at-the-seams full.

Measurement Conversions

BASIC KITCHEN CONVERSIONS & EQUIVALENTS

DRY MEASUREMENTS CONVERSION CHART

3 TEASPOONS = 1 TABLESPOON = 1/16 CUP

6 TEASPOONS = 2 TABLESPOONS = 1/8 CUP

12 TEASPOONS = 4 TABLESPOONS = 1/4 CUP

24 TEASPOONS = 8 TABLESPOONS = 1/2 CUP

36 TEASPOONS = 12 TABLESPOONS = 3/4 CUP

48 TEASPOONS = 16 TABLESPOONS = 1 CUP

METRIC TO US COOKING CONVERSIONS

OVEN TEMPERATURES

120 °C = 250 °F

160 °C = 320 °F

180° C = 350 °F

205 °C = 400 °F

220 °C = 425 °F

LIQUID MEASUREMENTS CONVERSION CHART

8 FLUID OUNCES = 1 CUP = 1/2 PINT = 1/4 QUART

16 FLUID OUNCES = 2 CUPS = 1 PINT = 1/2 QUART

32 FLUID OUNCES = 4 CUPS = 2 PINTS = 1 QUART = 1/4 GALLON

128 FLUID OUNCES = 16 CUPS = 8 PINTS = 4 QUARTS= 1 GALLON

BAKING IN GRAMS

1 CUP FLOUR = 140 GRAMS

1 CUP SUGAR = 150 GRAMS

1 CUP POWDERED SUGAR = 160 GRAMS

1 CUP HEAVY CREAM = 235 GRAMS

VOLUME

1 MILLILITER = 1/5 TEASPOON

5 ML = 1 TEASPOON

15 ML = 1 TABLESPOON

240 ML = 1 CUP OR 8 FLUID OUNCES

1 LITER = 34 FL. OUNCES

WEIGHT

1 GRAM = .035 OUNCES

100 GRAMS = 3.5 OUNCES

500 GRAMS = 1.1 POUNDS

1 KILOGRAM = 35 OUNCES

US TO METRIC COOKING CONVERSIONS

1/5 TSP = 1 ML

1 TSP = 5 ML

1 TBSP = 15 ML

1 FL OUNCE = 30 ML

1 CUP = 237 ML

1 PINT (2 CUPS) = 473 ML

1 QUART (4 CUPS) = .95 LITER

1 GALLON (16 CUPS) = 3.8 LITERS

1 OZ = 28 GRAMS

1 POUND = 454 GRAMS

BUTTER

1 CUP BUTTER = 2 STICKS = 8 OUNCES = 230 GRAMS = 8 TABLESPOONS

WHAT DOES 1 CUP EQUAL

1 CUP = 8 FLUID OUNCES

1 CUP = 16 TABLESPOONS

1 CUP = 48 TEASPOONS

1 CUP = 1/2 PINT

1 CUP = 1/4 QUART

1 CUP = 1/16 GALLON

1 CUP = 240 ML

BAKING PAN CONVERSIONS

1 CUP ALL-PURPOSE FLOUR = 4.5 OZ

1 CUP ROLLED OATS = 3 OZ 1 LARGE EGG = 1.7 OZ

1 CUP BUTTER = 8 OZ 1 CUP MILK = 8 OZ

1 CUP HEAVY CREAM = 8.4 OZ

1 CUP GRANULATED SUGAR = 7.1 OZ

1 CUP PACKED BROWN SUGAR = 7.75 OZ

1 CUP VEGETABLE OIL = 7.7 OZ

1 CUP UNSIFTED POWDERED SUGAR = 4.4 OZ

BAKING PAN CONVERSIONS

9-INCH ROUND CAKE PAN = 12 CUPS

10-INCH TUBE PAN =16 CUPS

11-INCH BUNDT PAN = 12 CUPS

9-INCH SPRINGFORM PAN = 10 CUPS

9 X 5 INCH LOAF PAN = 8 CUPS

9-INCH SQUARE PAN = 8 CUPS

Breakfast

Breakfast

Spinach Cheese Pie

Servings:8 | Cooking Time: 25 Minutes

Ingredients:
- 2 tablespoons extra-virgin olive oil
- 1 onion, chopped
- 1 pound frozen spinach, thawed
- ¼ teaspoon ground nutmeg
- ¼ teaspoon garlic salt
- ¼ teaspoon freshly ground black pepper
- 4 large eggs, divided
- 1 cup grated Parmesan cheese, divided
- 2 puff pastry doughs, at room temperature
- 4 hard-boiled eggs, halved
- Nonstick cooking spray

Directions:
1. Preheat the oven to 350ºF. Spritz a baking sheet with nonstick cooking spray and set aside.
2. Heat a large skillet over medium-high heat. Add the olive oil and onion and sauté for about 5 minutes, stirring occasionally, or until translucent.
3. Squeeze the excess water from the spinach, then add to the skillet and cook, uncovered, so that any excess water from the spinach can evaporate.
4. Season with the nutmeg, garlic salt, and black pepper. Remove from heat and set aside to cool.
5. Beat 3 eggs in a small bowl. Add the beaten eggs and ½ cup of Parmesan cheese to the spinach mixture, stirring well.
6. Roll out the pastry dough on the prepared baking sheet. Layer the spinach mixture on top of the dough, leaving 2 inches around each edge.
7. Once the spinach is spread onto the pastry dough, evenly place the hard-boiled egg halves throughout the pie, then cover with the second pastry dough. Pinch the edges closed.
8. Beat the remaining 1 egg in the bowl. Brush the egg wash over the pastry dough.
9. Bake in the preheated oven for 15 to 20 minutes until golden brown.
10. Sprinkle with the remaining ½ cup of Parmesan cheese. Cool for 5 minutes before cutting and serving.

Nutrition:
- Info Per Serving: Calories: 417;Fat: 28.0g;Protein: 17.0g;Carbs: 25.0g.

Sweet Banana Pancakes With Strawberries

Servings:4 | Cooking Time:15 Minutes

Ingredients:
- 2 tbsp olive oil
- 1 cup flour
- 1 cup + 2 tbsp milk
- 2 eggs, beaten
- ⅓ cup honey
- 1 tsp baking soda
- ¼ tsp salt
- 1 sliced banana
- 1 cup sliced strawberries
- 1 tbsp maple syrup

Directions:
1. Mix together the flour, milk, eggs, honey, baking soda, and salt in a bowl. Warm the olive oil in a skillet over medium heat and pour in ⅓ cup of the pancake batter. Cook for 2-3 minutes. Add half of the fresh fruit and flip to cook for 2-3 minutes on the other side until cooked through. Top with the remaining fruit, drizzle with maple syrup and serve.

Nutrition:
- Info Per Serving: Calories: 415;Fat: 24g;Protein: 12g;-Carbs: 46g.

Pecan & Peach Parfait

Servings:2 | Cooking Time:15 Minutes

Ingredients:
- 1 ½ cups Greek yogurt
- ½ cup pecans
- ½ cup whole-grain rolled oats
- 1 tsp honey
- 1 peeled and chopped peach
- Mint leaves for garnish

Directions:
1. Preheat oven to 310 °F. Pour the oats and pecans into a baking sheet and spread evenly. Toast for 11-13 minutes; set aside. Microwave honey for 30 seconds. Stir in the peach.
2. Divide some peach mixture between 2 glasses, spread some yogurt on top, and sprinkle with the oat mixture. Repeat the layering process to exhaust the ingredients, finishing with the peach mixture. Serve with mint leaves.

Nutrition:
- Info Per Serving: Calories: 403;Fat: 19g;Protein: 22g;-Carbs: 40g.

Avocado & Tuna Sandwiches

Servings:4 | Cooking Time:15 Minutes

Ingredients:
- 2 cans tuna, packed in olive oil
- 4 bun breads, sliced in half
- 2 tbsp garlic aioli
- 1 avocado, mashed
- 1 tbsp chopped capers
- 1 tsp chopped fresh cilantro

Directions:
1. Cut each round of bun in half and set aside. Add the tuna and oil into a bowl, and mix in the aioli, avocado, capers, and cilantro. Mix well with a fork. Toast the bread, remove and spread the tuna salad onto each quarter. Serve warm.

Nutrition:
- Info Per Serving: Calories: 436;Fat: 36g;Protein: 22.9g;-Carbs: 5g.

Carrot & Pecan Cupcakes

Servings:6 | Cooking Time:30 Minutes

Ingredients:
- 2 tbsp olive oil
- 1 ½ cups grated carrots
- ¼ cup pecans, chopped
- 1 cup oat bran
- 1 cup wholewheat flour
- ½ cup all-purpose flour
- ½ cup old-fashioned oats
- 3 tbsp light brown sugar
- 1 tsp vanilla extract
- ½ lemon, zested
- 1 tsp baking powder
- 2 tsp ground cinnamon
- 2 tsp ground ginger
- ½ tsp ground nutmeg
- ¼ tsp salt
- 1¼ cups soy milk
- 2 tbsp honey
- 1 egg

Directions:
1. Preheat oven to 350 °F. Mix whole-wheat flour, all-purpose flour, oat bran, oats, sugar, baking powder, cinnamon, nutmeg, ginger, and salt in a bowl; set aside.
2. Beat egg with soy milk, honey, vanilla, lemon zest, and olive oil in another bowl. Pour this mixture into the flour mixture and combine to blend, leaving some lumps. Stir in carrots and pecans. Spoon batter into greased muffin cups. Bake for about 20 minutes. Prick with a toothpick and if it comes out easily, the cakes are cooked done. Let cool and serve.

Nutrition:
- Info Per Serving: Calories: 346;Fat: 10g;Protein: 13g;-Carbs: 59g.

Tomato Scrambled Eggs With Feta Cheese

Servings:4 | Cooking Time:25 Minutes

Ingredients:
- ¼ cup olive oil
- 2 Roma tomatoes, chopped
- ¼ cup minced red onion
- 2 garlic cloves, minced
- ½ tsp dried oregano
- ½ tsp dried thyme
- 8 large eggs
- Salt and black pepper to taste
- ¾ cup feta cheese, crumbled
- ¼ cup fresh cilantro, chopped

Directions:
1. Warm the olive oil in a large skillet over medium heat. Add the chopped tomatoes and red onion and sauté for 10 minutes or until the tomatoes are soft. Add the garlic, oregano, and thyme and sauté for another 1-2 minutes until the liquid reduces.
2. In a medium bowl, whisk together the eggs, salt, and pepper until well combined. Add the eggs to the skillet, reduce the heat to low, and scramble until set and creamy, using a spatula to move them constantly, 3-4 minutes. Remove the skillet from the heat, stir in the feta and cilantro, and serve.

Nutrition:
- Info Per Serving: Calories: 338;Fat: 28g;Protein: 16g;-Carbs: 6g.

Morning Baklava French Toast

Servings:2 | Cooking Time:20 Minutes

Ingredients:
- 2 tbsp orange juice
- 3 fresh eggs, beaten
- 1 tsp lemon zest
- 1⁄8 tsp vanilla extract
- ¼ cup honey
- 2 tbsp whole milk
- ¾ tsp ground cinnamon
- ¼ cup walnuts, crumbled
- ¼ cup pistachios, crumbled
- 1 tbsp sugar
- 2 tbsp white bread crumbs
- 4 slices bread
- 2 tbsp unsalted butter

• 1 tsp confectioners' sugar

Directions:

1. Combine the eggs, orange juice, lemon zest, vanilla, honey, milk, and cinnamon in a bowl; set aside. Pulse walnuts and pistachios in a food processor until they are finely crumbled. In a small bowl, mix the walnuts, pistachios, sugar, and bread crumbs. Spread the nut mixture on 2 bread slices.

2. Cover with the remaining 2 slices. Melt the butter in a skillet over medium heat. Dip the sandwiches into the egg mixture and fry them for 4 minutes on both sides or until golden. Remove to a plate and cut them diagonally. Dust with confectioners' sugar. Serve immediately.

Nutrition:

• Info Per Serving: Calories: 651;Fat: 30g;Protein: 21g;-Carbs: 80g.

Easy Buckwheat Porridge

Servings:4 | Cooking Time: 40 Minutes

Ingredients:

• 3 cups water
• 2 cups raw buckwheat groats
• Pinch sea salt
• 1 cup unsweetened almond milk

Directions:

1. In a medium saucepan, add the water, buckwheat groats, and sea salt and bring to a boil over medium-high heat.

2. Once it starts to boil, reduce the heat to low. Cook for about 20 minutes, stirring occasionally, or until most of the water is absorbed.

3. Fold in the almond milk and whisk well. Continue cooking for about 15 minutes, or until the buckwheat groats are very softened.

4. Ladle the porridge into bowls and serve warm.

Nutrition:

• Info Per Serving: Calories: 121;Fat: 1.0g;Protein: 6.3g;-Carbs: 21.5g.

Kale Egg Cupcakes

Servings:2 | Cooking Time:40 Minutes

Ingredients:

• 1 whole-grain bread slice
• 4 large eggs, beaten
• 3 tbsp milk
• Salt and black pepper to taste
• ½ tsp onion powder
• ¼ tsp garlic powder
• ¾ cup chopped kale

Directions:

1. Heat the oven to 350 °F. Break the bread into pieces and

divide between 2 greased ramekins. Mix the eggs, milk, salt, onion powder, garlic powder, pepper, and kale in a medium bowl. Pour half of the egg mixture into each ramekin and bake for 25 minutes or until the eggs are set. Serve and enjoy!

Nutrition:

• Info Per Serving: Calories: 213;Fat: 12g;Protein: 17g;-Carbs: 13g.

Brown Rice And Black Bean Burgers

Servings:8 | Cooking Time: 40 Minutes

Ingredients:

• 1 cup cooked brown rice
• 1 can black beans, drained and rinsed
• 1 tablespoon olive oil
• 2 tablespoons taco or seasoning
• ½ yellow onion, finely diced
• 1 beet, peeled and grated
• 1 carrot, peeled and grated
• 2 tablespoons no-salt-added tomato paste
• 2 tablespoons apple cider vinegar
• 3 garlic cloves, minced
• ¼ teaspoon sea salt
• Ground black pepper, to taste
• 8 whole-wheat hamburger buns
• Toppings:
• 16 lettuce leaves, rinsed well
• 8 tomato slices, rinsed well
• Whole-grain mustard, to taste

Directions:

1. Line a baking sheet with parchment paper.

2. Put the brown rice and black beans in a food processor and pulse until mix well. Pour the mixture in a large bowl and set aside.

3. Heat the olive oil in a nonstick skillet over medium heat until shimmering.

4. Add the taco seasoning and stir for 1 minute or until fragrant.

5. Add the onion, beet, and carrot and sauté for 5 minutes or until the onion is translucent and beet and carrot are tender.

6. Pour in the tomato paste and vinegar, then add the garlic and cook for 3 minutes or until the sauce is thickened. Sprinkle with salt and ground black pepper.

7. Transfer the vegetable mixture to the bowl of rice mixture, then stir to mix well until smooth.

8. Divide and shape the mixture into 8 patties, then arrange the patties on the baking sheet and refrigerate for at least 1 hour.

9. Preheat the oven to 400ºF.

10. Remove the baking sheet from the refrigerator and allow to sit under room temperature for 10 minutes.

11. Bake in the preheated oven for 40 minutes or until golden brown on both sides. Flip the patties halfway through the cooking time.

12. Remove the patties from the oven and allow to cool for 10 minutes.

13. Assemble the buns with patties, lettuce, and tomato slices. Top the filling with mustard and serve immediately.

Nutrition:
• Info Per Serving: Calories: 544;Fat: 20.0g;Protein: 15.8g;Carbs: 76.0g.

Vegetable & Egg Sandwiches

Servings:2 | Cooking Time:15 Minutes

Ingredients:
• 1 Iceberg lettuce, separated into leaves
• 1 tbsp olive oil
• 1 tbsp butter
• 2 fontina cheese slices, grated
• 3 eggs
• 4 slices multigrain bread
• 3 radishes, sliced
• ½ cucumber, sliced
• 2 pimiento peppers, chopped
• Salt and red pepper to taste

Directions:
1. Warm the oil in a skillet over medium heat. Crack in the eggs and cook until the whites are set. Season with salt and red pepper; remove to a plate. Brush the bread slices with butter and toast them in the same skillet for 2 minutes per side.

2. Arrange 2 bread slices on a flat surface and put them over the eggs. Add in the remaining ingredients and top with the remaining slices. Serve immediately.

Nutrition:
• Info Per Serving: Calories: 487;Fat: 13g;Protein: 24g;-Carbs: 32g.

Cheesy Kale & Egg Cupcakes

Servings:2 | Cooking Time:30 Minutes

Ingredients:
• ¼ cup kale, chopped
• 3 eggs
• 1 leek, sliced
• 4 tbsp Parmesan, grated
• 2 tbsp almond milk
• 1 red bell pepper, chopped
• Salt and black pepper to taste
• 1 tomato, chopped
• 2 tbsp mozzarella, grated

Directions:

1. Preheat the oven to 360 F. Grease a muffin tin with cooking spray. Whisk the eggs in a bowl. Add in milk, kale, leek, Parmesan cheese, bell pepper, salt, black pepper, tomato, and mozzarella cheese and stir to combine. Divide the mixture between the cases and bake for 20-25 minutes. Let cool completely on a wire rack before serving.

Nutrition:
• Info Per Serving: Calories: 320;Fat: 20g;Protein: 26g;-Carbs: 9g.

Chickpea Lettuce Wraps

Servings:2 | Cooking Time: 0 Minutes

Ingredients:
• 1 can chickpeas, drained and rinsed well
• 1 celery stalk, diced
• ½ shallot, minced
• 1 green apple, cored and diced
• 3 tablespoons tahini (sesame paste)
• 2 teaspoons freshly squeezed lemon juice
• 1 teaspoon raw honey
• 1 teaspoon Dijon mustard
• Dash salt
• Filtered water, to thin
• 4 romaine lettuce leaves

Directions:
1. In a medium bowl, stir together the chickpeas, celery, shallot, apple, tahini, lemon juice, honey, mustard, and salt. If needed, add some water to thin the mixture.

2. Place the romaine lettuce leaves on a plate. Fill each with the chickpea filling, using it all. Wrap the leaves around the filling. Serve immediately.

Nutrition:
• Info Per Serving: Calories: 397;Fat: 15.1g;Protein: 15.1g;Carbs: 53.1g.

Red Pepper Coques With Pine Nuts

Servings:4 | Cooking Time: 45 Minutes

Ingredients:
• Dough:
• 3 cups almond flour
• ½ teaspoon instant or rapid-rise yeast
• 2 teaspoons raw honey
• 1⅓ cups ice water
• 3 tablespoons extra-virgin olive oil
• 1½ teaspoons sea salt
• Red Pepper Topping:
• 4 tablespoons extra-virgin olive oil, divided
• 2 cups jarred roasted red peppers, patted dry and sliced thinly
• 2 large onions, halved and sliced thin

- 3 garlic cloves, minced
- ¼ teaspoon red pepper flakes
- 2 bay leaves
- 3 tablespoons maple syrup
- 1½ teaspoons sea salt
- 3 tablespoons red whine vinegar
- For Garnish:
- ¼ cup pine nuts (optional)
- 1 tablespoon minced fresh parsley

Directions:
1. Make the Dough:
2. Combine the flour, yeast, and honey in a food processor, pulse to combine well. Gently add water while pulsing. Let the dough sit for 10 minutes.
3. Mix the olive oil and salt in the dough and knead the dough until smooth. Wrap in plastic and refrigerate for at least 1 day.
4. Make the Topping:
5. Heat 1 tablespoon of olive oil in a nonstick skillet over medium heat until shimmering.
6. Add the red peppers, onions, garlic, red pepper flakes, bay leaves, maple syrup, and salt. Sauté for 20 minutes or until the onion is caramelized.
7. Turn off the heat and discard the bay leaves. Remove the onion from the skillet and baste with wine vinegar. Let them sit until ready to use.
8. Make the Coques:
9. Preheat the oven to 500ºF. Grease two baking sheets with 1 tablespoon of olive oil.
10. Divide the dough ball into four balls, then press and shape them into equal-sized oval. Arrange the ovals on the baking sheets and pierce each dough about 12 times.
11. Rub the ovals with 2 tablespoons of olive oil and bake for 7 minutes or until puffed. Flip the ovals halfway through the cooking time.
12. Spread the ovals with the topping and pine nuts, then bake for an additional 15 minutes or until well browned.
13. Remove the coques from the oven and spread with parsley. Allow to cool for 10 minutes before serving.

Nutrition:
- Info Per Serving: Calories: 658;Fat: 23.1g;Protein: 3.4g;-Carbs: 112.0g.

Hot Egg Scramble

Servings:4 | Cooking Time:35 Minutes

Ingredients:
- 2 tbsp olive oil
- 1 small red onion, chopped
- 1 bell green pepper, chopped
- ½ tsp red pepper flakes
- 1 jalapeño, cut into strips
- 3 medium tomatoes, chopped

- Salt and black pepper to taste
- 1 tbsp ground cumin
- 1 tsp ground coriander
- 4 large eggs, lightly beaten

Directions:
1. Warm the olive oil in a skillet over medium heat. Add the onion and cook until soft and translucent, 5-7 minutes. Add the peppers and continue to cook for another 4-5 minutes until soft. Add in the tomatoes and season to taste. Stir in the cumin and coriander. Simmer for 10 minutes. Add the eggs, stirring them into the mixture to distribute. Cover the skillet and cook until the eggs are set but still fluffy and tender, 5-6 more minutes. Serve topped with red pepper flakes.

Nutrition:
- Info Per Serving: Calories: 171;Fat: 12.1g;Protein: 8.1g;-Carbs: 8g.

Almond Iced-coffee

Servings:1 | Cooking Time:5 Minutes

Ingredients:
- 1 cup brewed black coffee, warm
- 1 tbsp olive oil
- 1 tsp MCT oil
- 1 tbsp heavy cream
- ½ tsp almond extract
- ½ tsp ground cinnamon

Directions:
1. Pour the warm coffee (not hot) into a blender. Add the olive oil, heavy cream, MCT oil, almond extract, and cinnamon. Blend well until smooth and creamy. Drink warm and enjoy.

Nutrition:
- Info Per Serving: Calories: 128;Fat: 14.2g;Protein: 0g;-Carbs: 0g.

Falafel Balls With Tahini Sauce

Servings:4 | Cooking Time: 20 Minutes

Ingredients:
- Tahini Sauce:
- ½ cup tahini
- 2 tablespoons lemon juice
- ¼ cup finely chopped flat-leaf parsley
- 2 cloves garlic, minced
- ½ cup cold water, as needed
- Falafel:
- 1 cup dried chickpeas, soaked overnight, drained
- ¼ cup chopped flat-leaf parsley
- ¼ cup chopped cilantro
- 1 large onion, chopped

- 1 teaspoon cumin
- ½ teaspoon chili flakes
- 4 cloves garlic
- 1 teaspoon sea salt
- 5 tablespoons almond flour
- 1½ teaspoons baking soda, dissolved in 1 teaspoon water
- 2 cups peanut oil
- 1 medium bell pepper, chopped
- 1 medium tomato, chopped
- 4 whole-wheat pita breads

Directions:
1. Make the Tahini Sauce:
2. Combine the ingredients for the tahini sauce in a small bowl. Stir to mix well until smooth.
3. Wrap the bowl in plastic and refrigerate until ready to serve.
4. Make the Falafel:
5. Put the chickpeas, parsley, cilantro, onion, cumin, chili flakes, garlic, and salt in a food processor. Pulse to mix well but not puréed.
6. Add the flour and baking soda to the food processor, then pulse to form a smooth and tight dough.
7. Put the dough in a large bowl and wrap in plastic. Refrigerate for at least 2 hours to let it rise.
8. Divide and shape the dough into walnut-sized small balls.
9. Pour the peanut oil in a large pot and heat over high heat until the temperature of the oil reaches 375ºF.
10. Drop 6 balls into the oil each time, and fry for 5 minutes or until golden brown and crispy. Turn the balls with a strainer to make them fried evenly.
11. Transfer the balls on paper towels with the strainer, then drain the oil from the balls.
12. Roast the pita breads in the oven for 5 minutes or until golden brown, if needed, then stuff the pitas with falafel balls and top with bell peppers and tomatoes. Drizzle with tahini sauce and serve immediately.

Nutrition:
- Info Per Serving: Calories: 574;Fat: 27.1g;Protein: 19.8g;Carbs: 69.7g.

Grilled Caesar Salad Sandwiches

Servings:2 | Cooking Time: 5 Minutes

Ingredients:
- ¾ cup olive oil, divided
- 2 romaine lettuce hearts, left intact
- 3 to 4 anchovy fillets
- Juice of 1 lemon
- 2 to 3 cloves garlic, peeled
- 1 teaspoon Dijon mustard
- ¼ teaspoon Worcestershire sauce
- Sea salt and freshly ground pepper, to taste

- 2 slices whole-wheat bread, toasted
- Freshly grated Parmesan cheese, for serving

Directions:
1. Preheat the grill to medium-high heat and oil the grates.
2. On a cutting board, drizzle the lettuce with 1 to 2 tablespoons of olive oil and place on the grates.
3. Grill for 5 minutes, turning until lettuce is slightly charred on all sides. Let lettuce cool enough to handle.
4. In a food processor, combine the remaining olive oil with the anchovies, lemon juice, garlic, mustard, and Worcestershire sauce.
5. Pulse the ingredients until you have a smooth emulsion. Season with sea salt and freshly ground pepper to taste. Chop the lettuce in half and place on the bread.
6. Drizzle with the dressing and serve with a sprinkle of Parmesan cheese.

Nutrition:
- Info Per Serving: Calories: 949;Fat: 85.6g;Protein: 12.9g;Carbs: 34.1g.

Tomato & Prosciutto Sandwiches

Servings:4 | Cooking Time:10 Minutes

Ingredients:
- 1 large, ripe tomato, sliced into 8 rounds
- 8 whole-wheat bread slices
- 1 avocado, halved and pitted
- Salt and black pepper to taste
- 8 romaine lettuce leaves
- 8 thin prosciutto slices
- 1 tbsp cilantro, chopped

Directions:
1. Toast the bread and place on a large platter. Scoop the avocado flesh out of the skin into a small bowl. Season with pepper and salt. With a fork, gently mash the avocado until it resembles a creamy spread. Smear 4 bread slices with the avocado mix. Top with a layer of lettuce leaves, tomato slices, and prosciutto slices. Repeat the layers one more time, sprinkle with cilantro, then cover with the remaining bread slices. Serve and enjoy!

Nutrition:
- Info Per Serving: Calories: 262;Fat: 12.2g;Protein: 8g;-Carbs: 35g.

Parsley Tomato Eggs

Servings:6 | Cooking Time:25 Minutes

Ingredients:
- 2 tbsp olive oil
- 1 onion, chopped
- 2 garlic cloves, minced
- 2 cans tomatoes, diced
- 6 large eggs
- ½ cup fresh chives, chopped

Directions:
1. Warm the olive oil in a large skillet over medium heat. Add the onion and garlic and cook for 3 minutes, stirring occasionally. Pour in the tomatoes with their juices o and cook for 3 minutes until bubbling.
2. Crack one egg into a small custard cup. With a large spoon, make six indentations in the tomato mixture. Gently pour the first cracked egg into one indentation and repeat, cracking the remaining eggs, one at a time, into the custard cup and pouring one into each indentation. Cover the skillet and cook for 6-8 minutes. Top with chives and serve.

Nutrition:
- Info Per Serving: Calories: 123;Fat: 8g;Protein: 7g;-Carbs: 4g.

Pecorino Bulgur & Spinach Cupcakes

Servings:6 | Cooking Time:45 Minutes

Ingredients:
- 2 eggs, whisked
- 1 cup bulgur
- 3 cups water
- 1 cup spinach, torn
- 2 spring onions, chopped
- ¼ cup Pecorino cheese, grated
- ½ tsp garlic powder
- Sea salt and pepper to taste
- ½ tsp dried oregano

Directions:
1. Preheat the oven to 340 °F. Grease a muffin tin with cooking spray. Warm 2 cups of salted water in a saucepan over medium heat and add in bulgur. Bring to a boil and cook for 10-15 minutes. Remove to a bowl and fluff with a fork. Stir in spinach, spring onions, eggs, Pecorino cheese, garlic powder, salt, pepper, and oregano. Divide between muffin holes and bake for 25 minutes. Serve chilled.

Nutrition:
- Info Per Serving: Calories: 280;Fat: 12g;Protein: 5g;-Carbs: 9g.

Maple Peach Smoothie

Servings:2 | Cooking Time:5 Minutes

Ingredients:
- 2 cups almond milk
- 2 cups peaches, chopped
- 1 cup crushed ice
- ½ tsp ground ginger
- 1 tbsp maple syrup

Directions:
1. In a food processor, mix milk, peaches, ice, maple syrup, and ginger until smooth. Serve.

Nutrition:
- Info Per Serving: Calories: 639;Fat: 58g;Protein: 7g;-Carbs: 34.2g.

Garlic Bell Pepper Omelet

Servings:2 | Cooking Time:10 Minutes

Ingredients:
- 2 tbsp olive oil
- 2 red bell peppers, chopped
- ¼ tsp nutmeg
- 4 eggs, beaten
- 2 garlic cloves, crushed
- 1 tsp Italian seasoning

Directions:
1. Heat the oil in a skillet over medium heat. Stir-fry the peppers for 3 minutes or until lightly charred; reserve. Add the garlic to the skillet and sauté for 1 minute. Pour the eggs over the garlic, sprinkle with Italian seasoning and nutmeg, and cook for 2-3 minutes or until set. Using a spatula, loosen the edges and gently slide onto a plate. Add charred peppers and fold over. Serve hot.

Nutrition:
- Info Per Serving: Calories: 272;Fat: 22g;Protein: 12g;-Carbs: 6.4g.

Fluffy Almond Flour Pancakes With Strawberries

Servings:4 | Cooking Time: 15 Minutes

Ingredients:
- 1 cup plus 2 tablespoons unsweetened almond milk
- 1 cup almond flour
- 2 large eggs, whisked
- ⅓ cup honey
- 1 teaspoon baking soda
- ¼ teaspoon salt
- 2 tablespoons extra-virgin olive oil
- 1 cup sliced strawberries

Directions:
1. Combine the almond milk, almond flour, whisked eggs, honey, baking soda, and salt in a large bowl and whisk to incorporate.
2. Heat the olive oil in a large skillet over medium-high heat.
3. Make the pancakes: Pour ⅓ cup of batter into the hot skillet and swirl the pan so the batter covers the bottom evenly. Cook for 2 to 3 minutes until the pancake turns golden brown around the edges. Gently flip the pancake with a spatula and cook for 2 to 3 minutes until cooked through. Repeat with the remaining batter.
4. Serve the pancakes with the sliced strawberries on top.

Nutrition:
- Info Per Serving: Calories: 298;Fat: 11.7g;Protein: 11.8g;Carbs: 34.8g.

✓ Oven-baked Mozzarella Cheese Cups

Servings:2 | Cooking Time:20 Minutes

Ingredients:
- 2 eggs, whisked
- 1 tbsp chives, chopped
- 1 tbsp dill, chopped
- Salt and black pepper to taste
- 3 tbsp mozzarella, grated
- 1 tomato, chopped

Directions:
1. Preheat the oven to 400 °F. Grease 2 ramekins with cooking spray. Whisk eggs, tomato, mozzarella cheese, salt, pepper, dill, and chives in a bowl. Share into each ramekin and bake for 10 minutes. Serve warm.

Nutrition:
- Info Per Serving: Calories: 110;Fat: 8g;Protein: 8g;-Carbs: 3g.

✓ Cheese & Mushroom Muffins

Servings:6 | Cooking Time:40 Minutes

Ingredients:
- 6 eggs
- Salt and black pepper to taste
- 1 cup Gruyere cheese, grated
- 1 yellow onion, chopped
- 1 cup mushrooms, sliced
- ½ cup green olives, chopped

Directions:
1. Beat the eggs, salt, pepper, Gruyere cheese, onion, mushrooms, and green olives in a bowl. Pour into a silicone muffin tray and bake for 30 minutes at 360 F. Serve warm.

Nutrition:
- Info Per Serving: Calories: 120;Fat: 6g;Protein: 8g;-Carbs: 10g.

Napoli Scrambled Eggs With Anchovies

Servings:4 | Cooking Time:20 Minutes

Ingredients:
- 2 tbsp olive oil
- 1 green bell pepper, chopped
- 2 anchovy fillets, chopped
- 8 cherry tomatoes, cubed
- 2 spring onions, chopped
- 1 tbsp capers, drained
- 5 black olives, pitted and sliced
- 6 eggs, beaten
- Salt and black pepper to taste
- ¼ tsp dried oregano
- 1 tbsp parsley, chopped

Directions:
1. Warm the olive oil in a skillet over medium heat and cook the bell pepper and spring onions for 3 minutes. Add in anchovies, cherry tomatoes, capers, and black olives and cook for another 2 minutes. Stir in eggs and sprinkle with salt, pepper, and oregano and scramble for 5 minutes. Serve sprinkled with parsley.

Nutrition:
- Info Per Serving: Calories: 260;Fat: 18g;Protein: 12g;-Carbs: 12g.

Honey & Feta Frozen Yogurt

Servings:4 | Cooking Time:5 Minutes + Freezing Time

Ingredients:
- 1 tbsp honey
- 1 cup Greek yogurt
- ½ cup feta cheese, crumbled
- 2 tbsp mint leaves, chopped

Directions:

1. In a food processor, blend yogurt, honey, and feta cheese until smooth. Transfer to a wide dish, cover with plastic wrap, and put in the freezer for 2 hours or until solid. When frozen, spoon into cups, sprinkle with mint, and serve.

Nutrition:
- Info Per Serving: Calories: 170;Fat: 12g;Protein: 7g;-Carbs: 13g.

√Fresh Mozzarella & Salmon Frittata

Servings:4 | Cooking Time:15 Minutes

Ingredients:
- 1 ball fresh mozzarella cheese, chopped
- 2 tsp olive oil
- 8 fresh eggs
- ½ cup whole milk
- 1 spring onion, chopped
- ¼ cup chopped fresh basil
- Salt and black pepper to taste
- 3 oz smoked salmon, chopped

Directions:

1. Preheat your broiler to medium. Whisk the eggs with milk, spring onion, basil, pepper, and salt in a bowl. Heat the olive oil in a skillet over medium heat and pour in the egg mixture.

2. Top with mozzarella cheese and cook for 3–5 minutes until the frittata is set on the bottom and the egg is almost set but still moist on top. Scatter over the salmon and place the skillet under the preheated broiler for 1-2 minutes or until set and slightly puffed. Cut the frittata into wedges. Enjoy!

Nutrition:
- Info Per Serving: Calories: 351;Fat: 13g;Protein: 52g;-Carbs: 6g.

Cream Peach Smoothie

Servings:1 | Cooking Time:5 Minutes

Ingredients:
- 1 large peach, sliced
- 6 oz peach Greek yogurt
- 2 tbsp almond milk
- 2 ice cubes

Directions:

1. Blend the peach, yogurt, almond milk, and ice cubes in your food processor until thick and creamy. Serve and enjoy!

Nutrition:
- Info Per Serving: Calories: 228;Fat: 3g;Protein: 11g;-Carbs: 41.6g.

Power Green Smoothie

Servings:1 | Cooking Time:10 Minutes

Ingredients:
- 1 tbsp extra-virgin olive oil
- 1 avocado, peeled and pitted
- 1 cup milk
- ½ cup watercress
- ½ cup baby spinach leaves
- ½ cucumber, peeled and seeded
- 10 mint leaves, stems removed
- ½ lemon, juiced

Directions:

1. In a blender, mix avocado, milk, baby spinach, watercress, cucumber, olive oil, mint, and lemon juice and blend until smooth and creamy. Add more milk or water to achieve your desired consistency. Serve chilled or at room temperature.

Nutrition:
- Info Per Serving: Calories: 330;Fat: 30.2g;Protein: 4g;-Carbs: 19g.

Chia & Almond Oatmeal

Servings:2 | Cooking Time:10 Min + Chilling Time

Ingredients:
- ¼ tsp almond extract
- ½ cup milk
- ½ cup rolled oats
- 2 tbsp almonds, sliced
- 2 tbsp sugar
- 1 tsp chia seeds
- ¼ tsp ground cardamom
- ¼ tsp ground cinnamon

Directions:
1. Combine the milk, oats, almonds, sugar, chia seeds, cardamom, almond extract, and cinnamon in a mason jar and shake well. Keep in the refrigerator for 4 hours. Serve.

Nutrition:
- Info Per Serving: Calories: 131;Fat: 6.2g;Protein: 4.9g;-Carbs: 17g.

Creamy Breakfast Bulgur With Berries

Servings:2 | Cooking Time: 10 Minutes

Ingredients:
- ½ cup medium-grain bulgur wheat
- 1 cup water
- Pinch sea salt
- ¼ cup unsweetened almond milk
- 1 teaspoon pure vanilla extract
- ¼ teaspoon ground cinnamon
- 1 cup fresh berries of your choice

Directions:
1. Put the bulgur in a medium saucepan with the water and sea salt, and bring to a boil.
2. Cover, remove from heat, and let stand for 10 minutes until water is absorbed.
3. Stir in the milk, vanilla, and cinnamon until fully incorporated. Divide between 2 bowls and top with the fresh berries to serve.

Nutrition:
- Info Per Serving: Calories: 173;Fat: 1.6g;Protein: 5.7g;-Carbs: 34.0g.

Almond Grits With Honey

Servings:4 | Cooking Time:15 Minutes

Ingredients:
- ¼ cup slivered almonds
- ½ cup milk
- ½ tsp almond extract
- ½ cup quick-cooking grits
- ½ tsp ground cinnamon
- ¼ cup honey
- ¼ tsp sea salt

Directions:
1. Bring to a boil the milk, salt, and 1 ½ cups of water in a pot over medium heat. Gradually add in grits, stirring constantly. Lower the heat and simmer for 6 minutes until all the liquid is absorbed. Mix in almond extract and cinnamon and cook for another minute. Ladle into individual bowls, top with almonds and honey, and serve. Enjoy!

Nutrition:
- Info Per Serving: Calories: 131;Fat: 3.8g;Protein: 2.6g;-Carbs: 23g.

Eggs Florentine With Pancetta

Servings:2 | Cooking Time:20 Minutes

Ingredients:
- 1 English muffin, toasted and halved
- ¼ cup chopped pancetta
- 2 tsp hollandaise sauce
- 1 cup spinach
- Salt and black pepper to taste
- 2 large eggs

Directions:
1. Place pancetta in a pan over medium heat and cook for 5 minutes until crispy; reserve. Add the baby spinach and cook for 2-3 minutes in the same pan until the spinach wilts. Fill a pot with 3 inches of water over medium heat and bring to a boil. Add 1 tbsp of vinegar and reduce the heat.
2. Crack the eggs one at a time into a small dish and gently pour into the simmering water. Poach the eggs for 2-3 minutes until the whites are set, but the yolks are still soft; remove with a slotted spoon. Divide the spinach between muffin halves and top with pancetta and poached eggs. Spoon the hollandaise sauce on top and serve.

Nutrition:
- Info Per Serving: Calories: 173;Fat: 7g;Protein: 11g;-Carbs: 17g.

Basic Tortilla De Patatas

Servings:4 | Cooking Time:35 Minutes

Ingredients:
- 1 ½ lb gold potatoes, peeled and sliced
- ½ cup olive oil
- 1 sweet onion, thinly sliced
- 8 eggs
- ½ dried oregano
- Salt to taste

Directions:
1. Heat the olive oil in a skillet over medium heat. Fry the potatoes for 8-10 minutes, stirring often. Add in onion, oregano, and salt and cook for 5-6 minutes until the potatoes are tender and slightly golden; set aside.
2. In a bowl, beat the eggs with a pinch of salt. Add in the potato mixture and mix well. Pour into the skillet and cook for about 10-12 minutes. Flip the tortilla using a plate, and cook for 2 more minutes until nice and crispy. Slice and serve.

Nutrition:
- Info Per Serving: Calories: 440;Fat: 34g;Protein: 14g;-Carbs: 22g.

Banana & Chocolate Porridge

Servings:4 | Cooking Time:20 Minutes

Ingredients:
- 2 bananas
- 4 dried apricots, chopped
- 1 cup barley, soaked
- 2 tbsp flax seeds
- 1 tbsp cocoa powder
- 1 cup coconut milk
- ¼ tsp mint leaves
- 2 oz dark chocolate bars, grated
- 2 tbsp coconut flakes

Directions:
1. Place the barley in a saucepan along with the flaxseeds and two cups of water. Bring to a boil, then lower the heat and simmer for 12 minutes, stirring often.
2. Meanwhile, in a food processor, blend bananas, cocoa powder, coconut milk, apricots, and mint leaves until smooth. Once the barley is ready, stir in chocolate. Add in banana mixture. Garnish with coconut flakes. Serve.

Nutrition:
- Info Per Serving: Calories: 476;Fat: 22g;Protein: 10g;-Carbs: 65g.

Spicy Tofu Tacos With Cherry Tomato Salsa

Servings:4 | Cooking Time: 11 Minutes

Ingredients:
- Cherry Tomato Salsa:
- ¼ cup sliced cherry tomatoes
- ½ jalapeño, deseeded and sliced
- Juice of 1 lime
- 1 garlic clove, minced
- Sea salt and freshly ground black pepper, to taste
- 2 teaspoons extra-virgin olive oil
- Spicy Tofu Taco Filling:
- 4 tablespoons water, divided
- ½ cup canned black beans, rinsed and drained
- 2 teaspoons fresh chopped chives, divided
- ¾ teaspoon ground cumin, divided
- ¾ teaspoon smoked paprika, divided
- Dash cayenne pepper (optional)
- ¼ teaspoon sea salt
- ¼ teaspoon freshly ground black pepper
- 1 teaspoon extra-virgin olive oil
- 6 ounces firm tofu, drained, rinsed, and pressed
- 4 corn tortillas
- ¼ avocado, sliced
- ¼ cup fresh cilantro

Directions:
1. Make the Cherry Tomato Salsa:
2. Combine the ingredients for the salsa in a small bowl. Stir to mix well. Set aside until ready to use.
3. Make the Spicy Tofu Taco Filling:
4. Add 2 tablespoons of water into a saucepan, then add the black beans and sprinkle with 1 teaspoon of chives, ½ teaspoon of cumin, ¼ teaspoon of smoked paprika, and cayenne. Stir to mix well.
5. Cook for 5 minutes over medium heat until heated through, then mash the black beans with the back of a spoon. Turn off the heat and set aside.
6. Add remaining water into a bowl, then add the remaining chives, cumin, and paprika. Sprinkle with cayenne, salt, and black pepper. Stir to mix well. Set aside.
7. Heat the olive oil in a nonstick skillet over medium heat until shimmering.
8. Add the tofu and drizzle with taco sauce, then sauté for 5 minutes or until the seasoning is absorbed. Remove the tofu from the skillet and set aside.
9. Warm the tortillas in the skillet for 1 minutes or until heated through.
10. Transfer the tortillas onto a large plate and top with tofu, mashed black beans, avocado, cilantro, then drizzle the tomato salsa over. Serve immediately.

Nutrition:
- Info Per Serving: Calories: 240;Fat: 9.0g;Protein: 11.6g;-Carbs: 31.6g.

Classic Shakshuka

Servings:2 | Cooking Time: 30 Minutes

Ingredients:

- 1 tablespoon olive oil
- ½ red pepper, diced
- ½ medium onion, diced
- 2 small garlic cloves, minced
- ½ teaspoon smoked paprika
- ½ teaspoon cumin
- Pinch red pepper flakes
- 1 can fire-roasted tomatoes
- ¼ teaspoon salt
- Pinch freshly ground black pepper
- 1 ounce crumbled feta cheese (about ¼ cup)
- 3 large eggs
- 3 tablespoons minced fresh parsley

Directions:

1. Heat the olive oil in a skillet over medium-high heat and add the pepper, onion, and garlic. Sauté until the vegetables start to turn golden.

2. Add the paprika, cumin, and red pepper flakes and stir to toast the spices for about 30 seconds. Add the tomatoes with their juices.

3. Reduce the heat and let the sauce simmer for 10 minutes, or until it starts to thicken. Add the salt and pepper. Taste the sauce and adjust seasonings as necessary.

4. Scatter the feta cheese on top. Make 3 wells in the sauce and crack one egg into each well.

5. Cover and let the eggs cook for about 7 minutes. Remove the lid and continue cooking for 5 minutes more, or until the yolks are cooked to desired doneness.

6. Garnish with fresh parsley and serve.

Nutrition:

- Info Per Serving: Calories: 289;Fat: 18.2g;Protein: 15.1g;Carbs: 18.5g.

Classic Socca

Servings:4 | Cooking Time: 10 Minutes

Ingredients:

- 1½ cups chickpea flour
- ½ teaspoon ground turmeric
- ½ teaspoon sea salt
- ½ teaspoon ground black pepper
- 2 tablespoons plus 2 teaspoons extra-virgin olive oil
- 1½ cups water

Directions:

1. Combine the chickpea flour, turmeric, salt, and black pepper in a bowl. Stir to mix well, then gently mix in 2 tablespoons of olive oil and water. Stir to mix until smooth.

2. Heat 2 teaspoons of olive oil in an 8-inch nonstick skillet over medium-high heat until shimmering.

3. Add half cup of the mixture into the skillet and swirl the skillet so the mixture coat the bottom evenly.

4. Cook for 5 minutes or until lightly browned and crispy. Flip the socca halfway through the cooking time. Repeat with the remaining mixture.

5. Slice and serve warm.

Nutrition:

- Info Per Serving: Calories: 207;Fat: 10.2g;Protein: 7.9g;-Carbs: 20.7g.

Poultry And Meats

Poultry And Meats

Slow Cooker Beef Stew

Servings:4 | Cooking Time:8 Hours 10 Minutes

Ingredients:
- 2 tbsp canola oil
- 2 lb beef stew meat, cubed
- Salt and black pepper to taste
- 2 cups beef stock
- 2 shallots, chopped
- 2 tbsp thyme, chopped
- 2 garlic cloves, minced
- 1 carrot, chopped
- 3 celery stalks, chopped
- 28 oz canned tomatoes, diced
- 2 tbsp parsley, chopped

Directions:
1. Place the beef meat, salt, pepper, beef stock, canola oil, shallots, thyme, garlic, carrot, celery, and tomatoes in your slow cooker. Put the lid and cook for 8 hours on Low. Sprinkle with parsley and serve warm.

Nutrition:
- Info Per Serving: Calories: 370;Fat: 17g;Protein: 35g;-Carbs: 28g.

Balsamic Chicken Breasts With Feta

Servings:4 | Cooking Time:35 Minutes

Ingredients:
- 1 lb chicken breasts, cut into strips
- 2 tbsp olive oil
- 1 fennel bulb, chopped
- Salt and black pepper to taste
- 2 tbsp balsamic vinegar
- 2 cups tomatoes, cubed
- 1 tbsp chives, chopped
- ¼ cup feta cheese, crumbled

Directions:
1. Warm the olive oil in a skillet over medium heat and sear chicken for 5 minutes, stirring often. Mix in fennel, salt, pepper, vinegar, and tomatoes and cook for 20 minutes. Top with feta cheese and chives and serve.

Nutrition:
- Info Per Serving: Calories: 290;Fat: 16g;Protein: 15g;-Carbs: 16g.

Pork Chops In Tomato Olive Sauce

Servings:4 | Cooking Time:20 Minutes

Ingredients:
- 2 tbsp olive oil
- 4 pork loin chops, boneless
- 6 tomatoes, crushed
- 3 tbsp basil, chopped
- 10 black olives, halved
- 1 yellow onion, chopped
- 1 garlic clove, minced

Directions:
1. Warm the olive oil in a skillet over medium heat and brown pork chops for 6 minutes on all sides. Share into plates. In the same skillet, stir tomatoes, basil, olives, onion, and garlic and simmer for 4 minutes. Drizzle tomato sauce over.

Nutrition:
- Info Per Serving: Calories: 340;Fat: 18g;Protein: 35g;-Carbs: 13g.

Saucy Turkey With Ricotta Cheese

Servings:4 | Cooking Time:60 Minutes

Ingredients:
- 2 tbsp olive oil
- 1 turkey breast, cubed
- 1 ½ cups salsa verde
- Salt and black pepper to taste
- 4 oz ricotta cheese, crumbled
- 2 tbsp cilantro, chopped

Directions:
1. Preheat the oven to 380° F. Grease a roasting pan with oil. In a bowl, place turkey, salsa verde, salt, and pepper and toss to coat. Transfer to the roasting pan and bake for 50 minutes. Top with ricotta cheese and cilantro and serve.

Nutrition:
- Info Per Serving: Calories: 340;Fat: 16g;Protein: 35g;-Carbs: 23g.

Eggplant & Chicken Skillet

Servings:4 | Cooking Time:40 Minutes

Ingredients:
- 2 tbsp olive oil
- 1 lb eggplants, cubed
- Salt and black pepper to taste
- 1 onion, chopped
- 2 garlic cloves, minced
- 1 tsp hot paprika
- 1 tbsp oregano, chopped
- 1 cup chicken stock
- 1 lb chicken breasts, cubed
- 1 cup half and half
- 3 tsp toasted chopped almonds

Directions:
1. Warm the olive oil in a skillet over medium heat and sauté chicken for 8 minutes, stirring often. Mix in eggplants, onion, and garlic and cook for another 5 minutes. Season with salt, pepper, hot paprika, and oregano and pour in the stock. Bring to a boil and simmer for 16 minutes. Stir in half and half for 2 minutes. Serve topped with almonds.

Nutrition:
- Info Per Serving: Calories: 400;Fat: 13g;Protein: 26g;- Carbs: 22g.

Tender Pork Shoulder

Servings:4 | Cooking Time:2 Hours 10 Minutes

Ingredients:
- 3 tbsp olive oil
- 2 lb pork shoulder
- 1 onion, chopped
- 2 tbsp garlic, minced
- 1 tbsp hot paprika
- 1 tbsp basil, chopped
- 1 cup chicken broth
- Salt and black pepper to taste

Directions:
1. Preheat oven to 350° F. Heat olive oil in a skillet and brown the pork on all sides for about 8-10 minutes; remove to a baking dish. Add onion and garlic to the skillet and sauté for 3 minutes until softened. Stir in hot paprika, salt, and pepper for 1 minute and pour in chicken broth. Transfer to the baking dish, cover with aluminium foil and bake for 90 minutes. Then remove the foil and continue baking for another 20 minutes until browned on top. Let the pork cool for a few minutes, slice, and sprinkle with basil. Serve topped with the cooking juices.

Nutrition:
- Info Per Serving: Calories: 310;Fat: 15g;Protein: 18g;- Carbs: 21g.

Tunisian Baharaat Grilled Chicken

Servings:4 | Cooking Time:20 Min + Marinating Time

Ingredients:
- 2 tbsp olive oil
- ¼ cup apple cider vinegar
- 1 lemon, zested and juiced
- 4 cloves garlic, minced
- 2 tsp sea salt
- ½ tsp chili powder
- 1 tsp Arabic 7 spices (baharaat)
- ½ tsp cinnamon
- 1 lb chicken breasts

Directions:
1. In a shallow dish, whisk the olive oil, vinegar, lemon juice, lemon zest, garlic, salt, baharaat, chili powder, and cinnamon. Add the chicken and toss to coat. Marinate for 1 hour. Next, drain, reserving the marinade.
2. Heat your grill to medium-high. Cook the chicken for 10-14 minutes, brushing them with the marinade every 5 minutes until the chicken is golden brown. Serve and enjoy!

Nutrition:
- Info Per Serving: Calories: 516;Fat: 33g;Protein: 49g;- Carbs: 2.5g.

Herby Turkey Stew

Servings:4 | Cooking Time:60 Minutes

Ingredients:
- 1 skinless, boneless turkey breast, cubed
- 2 tbsp olive oil
- Salt and black pepper to taste
- 1 tbsp sweet paprika
- ½ cup chicken stock
- 1 lb pearl onions
- 2 garlic cloves, minced
- 1 carrot, sliced
- 1 tsp cumin, ground
- 1 tbsp basil, chopped
- 1 tbsp cilantro, chopped

Directions:
1. Warm the olive oil in a pot over medium heat and sear turkey for 8 minutes, stirring occasionally. Stir in pearl onions, carrot, and garlic and cook for another 3 minutes. Season with salt, pepper, cumin, and paprika. Pour in the stock and bring to a boil; cook for 40 minutes. Top with basil and cilantro.

Nutrition:
- Info Per Serving: Calories: 260;Fat: 12g;Protein: 19g;- Carbs: 24g.

Greek-Style Lamb Burgers

Servings:4 | Cooking Time: 10 Minutes

Ingredients:
- 1 pound ground lamb
- ½ teaspoon salt
- ½ teaspoon freshly ground black pepper
- 4 tablespoons crumbled feta cheese
- Buns, toppings, and tzatziki, for serving (optional)

Directions:
1. Preheat the grill to high heat.
2. In a large bowl, using your hands, combine the lamb with the salt and pepper.
3. Divide the meat into 4 portions. Divide each portion in half to make a top and a bottom. Flatten each half into a 3-inch circle. Make a dent in the center of one of the halves and place 1 tablespoon of the feta cheese in the center. Place the second half of the patty on top of the feta cheese and press down to close the 2 halves together, making it resemble a round burger.
4. Grill each side for 3 minutes, for medium-well. Serve on a bun with your favorite toppings and tzatziki sauce, if desired.

Nutrition:
- Info Per Serving: Calories: 345;Fat: 29.0g;Protein: 20.0g;Carbs: 1.0g.

Portuguese-Style Chicken Breasts

Servings:4 | Cooking Time:45 Minutes

Ingredients:
- 2 tbsp avocado oil
- 1 lb chicken breasts, cubed
- Salt and black pepper to taste
- 1 red onion, chopped
- 15 oz canned chickpeas
- 15 oz canned tomatoes, diced
- 1 cup Kalamata olives, pitted and halved
- 2 tbsp lime juice
- 1 tsp cilantro, chopped

Directions:
1. Warm the olive oil in a pot over medium heat and sauté chicken and onion for 5 minutes. Put in salt, pepper, chickpeas, tomatoes, olives, lime juice, cilantro, and 2 cups of water. Cover with lid and bring to a boil, then reduce the heat and simmer for 30 minutes. Serve warm.

Nutrition:
- Info Per Serving: Calories: 360;Fat: 16g;Protein: 28g;-Carbs: 26g.

Cilantro Turkey Penne With Asparagus

Servings:4 | Cooking Time:40 Minutes

Ingredients:
- 3 tbsp olive oil
- 16 oz penne pasta
- 1 lb turkey breast strips
- 1 lb asparagus, chopped
- 1 tsp basil, chopped
- Salt and black pepper to taste
- ½ cup tomato sauce
- 2 tbsp cilantro, chopped

Directions:
1. Bring to a boil salted water in a pot over medium heat and cook penne until "al dente", 8-10 minutes. Drain and set aside; reserve 1 cup of the cooking water.
2. Warm the olive oil in a skillet over medium heat and sear turkey for 4 minutes, stirring periodically. Add in asparagus and sauté for 3-4 more minutes. Pour in the tomato sauce and reserved pasta liquid and bring to a boil; simmer for 20 minutes. Stir in cooked penne, season with salt and pepper, and top with the basil and cilantro to serve.

Nutrition:
- Info Per Serving: Calories: 350;Fat: 22g;Protein: 19g;-Carbs: 23g.

Spinach-Cheese Stuffed Pork Loin

Servings:6 | Cooking Time:55 Minutes

Ingredients:
- 1 ½ lb pork tenderloin
- 6 slices pancetta, chopped
- 1 cup mushrooms, sliced
- 5 sundried tomatoes, diced
- Salt and black pepper to taste

Directions:
1. Place a skillet over medium heat and stir-fry the pancetta for 5 minutes until crispy. Add the mushrooms and sauté for another 4-5 minutes until tender, stirring occasionally. Stir in sundried tomatoes and season with salt and pepper; set aside. Preheat the oven to 350°F. Using a sharp knife, cut the pork tenderloin in half lengthwise, leaving about 1-inch border; be careful not to cut through to the other side. Open the tenderloin like a book to form a large rectangle.
2. Flatten it to about ¼-inch thickness with a meat tenderizer. Season the pork generously with salt and pepper. Top all over with pancetta filling. Roll up pork tenderloin and tightly secure with kitchen twine. Place on a greased baking sheet. Bake for 60-75 minutes until the pork is cooked through, depending on the thickness of the pork. Remove from the oven and let rest for 10 minutes at room temperature. Remove the twine and discard. Slice the pork into

medallions and serve.

Nutrition:
• Info Per Serving: Calories: 270;Fat: 21g;Protein: 20g;-Carbs: 2g.

Thyme Zucchini & Chicken Stir-Fry

Servings:4 | Cooking Time:40 Minutes

Ingredients:
• 2 tbsp olive oil
• 2 cups tomatoes, crushed
• 1 lb chicken breasts, cubed
• Salt and black pepper to taste
• 2 shallots, sliced
• 3 garlic cloves, minced
• 2 zucchinis, sliced
• 2 tbsp thyme, chopped
• 1 cup chicken stock

Directions:
1. Warm the olive oil in a skillet over medium heat. Sear chicken for 6 minutes, stirring occasionally. Add in shallots and garlic and cook for another 4 minutes. Stir in tomatoes, salt, pepper, zucchinis, and stock and bring to a boil; simmer for 20 minutes. Garnish with thyme and serve.

Nutrition:
• Info Per Serving: Calories: 240;Fat: 10g;Protein: 19g;-Carbs: 17g.

Spinach Chicken With Chickpeas

Servings:4 | Cooking Time:25 Minutes

Ingredients:
• 2 tbsp olive oil
• 1 lb chicken breasts, cubed
• 10 oz spinach, chopped
• 1 cup canned chickpeas
• 1 onion, chopped
• 2 garlic cloves, minced
• ½ cup chicken stock
• 2 tbsp Parmesan cheese, grated
• 1 tbsp parsley, chopped
• Salt and black pepper to taste

Directions:
1. Warm the olive oil in a skillet over medium heat and brown chicken for 5 minutes. Season with salt and pepper. Stir in onion and garlic for 3 minutes. Pour in stock and chickpeas and bring to a boil. Cook for 20 minutes. Mix in spinach and cook until wilted, about 5 minutes. Top with Parmesan cheese and parsley. Serve and enjoy!

Nutrition:
• Info Per Serving: Calories: 290;Fat: 10g;Protein: 35g;-Carbs: 22g.

Spinach-ricotta Chicken Rolls

Servings:4 | Cooking Time:55 Minutes

Ingredients:
• 2 tbsp olive oil
• 4 chicken breast halves
• 1 lb baby spinach
• 2 garlic cloves, minced
• 1 lemon, zested
• ½ cup crumbled ricotta cheese
• 1 tbsp pine nuts, toasted
• Salt and black pepper to taste

Directions:
1. Preheat oven to 350° F. Pound the chicken breasts to ½-inch thickness with a meat mallet and season with salt and pepper.
2. Warm olive oil in a pan over medium heat and sauté spinach for 4-5 minutes until it wilts. Stir in garlic, salt, lemon zest, and pepper for 20-30 seconds. Let cool slightly and add in ricotta cheese and pine nuts; mix well. Spoon the mixture over the chicken breasts, wrap around the filling, and secure the ends with toothpicks. Arrange the breasts on a greased baking dish and bake for 35-40 minutes. Let sit for a few minutes and slice. Serve immediately.

Nutrition:
• Info Per Serving: Calories: 260;Fat: 14g;Protein: 28g;-Carbs: 6.5g.

Date Lamb Tangine

Servings:4 | Cooking Time:40 Minutes

Ingredients:
• 2 tbsp olive oil
• 1 tbsp dates, chopped
• 1 lb lamb, cubed
• 1 garlic clove, minced
• 1 onion, grated
• 2 tbsp orange juice
• Salt and black pepper to taste
• 1 cup vegetable stock

Directions:
1. Warm the olive oil in a skillet over medium heat and cook onion and garlic for 5 minutes. Put in lamb and cook for another 5 minutes. Stir in dates, orange juice, salt, pepper, and stock and bring to a boil; cook for 20 minutes. Serve.

Nutrition:
• Info Per Serving: Calories: 298;Fat: 14g;Protein: 17g;-Carbs: 19g.

Tzatziki Chicken Loaf

Servings:4 | Cooking Time:70 Min + Chilling Time

Ingredients:
- 1 lb ground chicken
- 1 onion, chopped
- 1 tsp garlic powder
- 1 cup tzatziki sauce
- ½ tsp dried Greek oregano
- ½ tsp dried cilantro
- ½ tsp sweet paprika
- Salt and black pepper to taste

Directions:

1. Preheat oven to 350° F. In a bowl, add chicken, paprika, onion, Greek oregano, cilantro, garlic, salt, and pepper and mix well with your hands. Shape the mixture into a greased loaf pan and bake in the oven for 55-60 minutes. Let sit for 15 minutes and slice. Serve topped with tzatziki sauce.

Nutrition:
- Info Per Serving: Calories: 240;Fat: 9g;Protein: 33.2g;-Carbs: 3.6g.

Ground Beef, Tomato, And Kidney Bean Chili

Servings:4 | Cooking Time: 15 Minutes

Ingredients:
- 1 tablespoon extra-virgin olive oil
- 1 pound extra-lean ground beef
- 1 onion, chopped
- 2 cans kidney beans
- 2 cans chopped tomatoes, juice reserved
- Simple Chili Spice:
- 1 teaspoon garlic powder
- 1 tablespoon chili powder
- ½ teaspoon sea salt

Directions:

1. Heat the olive oil in a pot over medium-high heat until shimmering.

2. Add the beef and onion to the pot and sauté for 5 minutes or until the beef is lightly browned and the onion is translucent.

3. Add the remaining ingredients. Bring to a boil. Reduce the heat to medium and cook for 10 more minutes. Keep stirring during the cooking.

4. Pour them in a large serving bowl and serve immediately.

Nutrition:
- Info Per Serving: Calories: 891;Fat: 20.1g;Protein: 116.3g;Carbs: 62.9g.

Mustardy Steak In Mushroom Sauce

Servings:4 | Cooking Time:30 Min + Marinating Time

Ingredients:
- For the steak
- 2 tbsp olive oil
- 1 lb beef skirt steak
- 1 cup red wine
- 2 garlic cloves, minced
- 1 tbsp Worcestershire sauce
- 1 tbsp dried thyme
- 1 tsp yellow mustard
- For the mushroom sauce
- 1 lb mushrooms, sliced
- 1 tsp dried dill
- 2 garlic cloves, minced
- 1 cup dry red wine
- Salt and black pepper to taste

Directions:

1. Combine wine, garlic, Worcestershire sauce, 2 tbsp of olive oil, thyme, and mustard in a bowl. Place in the steak, cover with plastic wrap and let it marinate for at least 3 hours in the refrigerator. Remove the steak and pat dry with paper towels.

2. Warm olive oil in a pan over medium heat and sear steak for 8 minutes on all sides; set aside. In the same pan, sauté mushrooms, dill, salt, and pepper for 6 minutes, stirring periodically. Add in garlic and sauté for 30 seconds. Pour in the wine and scrape off any bits from the bottom. Simmer for 5 minutes until the liquid reduces. Slice the steak and top with the mushroom sauce. Serve hot.

Nutrition:
- Info Per Serving: Calories: 424;Fat: 24g;Protein: 29g;-Carbs: 8g.

Chicken Cacciatore

Servings:2 | Cooking Time: 1 Hour And 30 Minutes

Ingredients:
- 1½ pounds bone-in chicken thighs, skin removed and patted dry
- Salt, to taste
- 2 tablespoons olive oil
- ½ large onion, thinly sliced
- 4 ounces baby bella mushrooms, sliced
- 1 red sweet pepper, cut into 1-inch pieces
- 1 can crushed fire-roasted tomatoes
- 1 fresh rosemary sprig
- ½ cup dry red wine
- 1 teaspoon Italian herb seasoning
- ½ teaspoon garlic powder
- 3 tablespoons flour

Directions:
1. Season the chicken thighs with a generous pinch of salt.
2. Heat the olive oil in a Dutch oven over medium-high heat. Add the chicken and brown for 5 minutes per side.
3. Add the onion, mushrooms, and sweet pepper to the Dutch oven and sauté for another 5 minutes.
4. Add the tomatoes, rosemary, wine, Italian seasoning, garlic powder, and salt, stirring well.
5. Bring the mixture to a boil, then reduce the heat to low. Allow to simmer slowly for at least 1 hour, stirring occasionally, or until the chicken is tender and easily pulls away from the bone.
6. Measure out 1 cup of the sauce from the pot and put it into a bowl. Add the flour and whisk well to make a slurry.
7. Increase the heat to medium-high and slowly whisk the slurry into the pot. Stir until it comes to a boil and cook until the sauce is thickened.
8. Remove the chicken from the bones and shred it, and add it back to the sauce before serving, if desired.

Nutrition:
- Info Per Serving: Calories: 520;Fat: 23.1g;Protein: 31.8g;Carbs: 37.0g.

Zesty Turkey Breast

Servings:4 | Cooking Time:1 Hr 40 Min + Chilling Time

Ingredients:
- 2 tbsp olive oil
- 1 lb turkey breast
- 2 garlic cloves, minced
- ½ cup chicken broth
- 1 lemon, zested
- ¼ tsp dried thyme
- ¼ tsp dried tarragon
- ½ tsp red pepper flakes
- 2 tbsp chopped fresh parsley
- 1 tsp ground mustard
- Salt and black pepper to taste

Directions:
1. Preheat oven to 325° F. Mix the olive oil, garlic, lemon zest, thyme, tarragon, red pepper flakes, mustard, salt, and pepper in a bowl. Rub the breast with the mixture until well coated and transfer onto a roasting pan skin-side up. Pour in the chicken broth. Roast in the oven for 60-90 minutes. Allow to sit for 10 minutes covered with foil, then remove from the roasting tin and carve. Serve topped with parsley.

Nutrition:
- Info Per Serving: Calories: 286;Fat: 16g;Protein: 34g;-Carbs: 0.9g.

Tasty Chicken Pot

Servings:4 | Cooking Time:35 Minutes

Ingredients:
- 1 lb chicken thighs, skinless and boneless
- 2 tbsp olive oil
- 1 onion, chopped
- 2 garlic cloves, minced
- 1 tsp smoked paprika
- 1 tsp chili powder
- ½ tsp fennel seeds, ground
- 2 tsp oregano, dried
- 14 oz canned tomatoes, diced
- ½ cup capers

Directions:
1. Warm the olive oil in a skillet over medium heat and sauté the onion, garlic, paprika, chili powder, fennel seeds, and oregano for 3 minutes. Put in chicken, tomatoes, 1 cup of water, and capers. Bring to a boil and simmer for 20-25 minutes.

Nutrition:
- Info Per Serving: Calories: 160;Fat: 9g;Protein: 13g;-Carbs: 10g.

Rich Pork In Cilantro Sauce

Servings:4 | Cooking Time:30 Minutes

Ingredients:
- ½ cup olive oil
- 1 lb pork stew meat, cubed
- 1 tbsp walnuts, chopped
- 2 tbsp cilantro, chopped
- 2 tbsp basil, chopped
- 2 garlic cloves, minced
- Salt and black pepper to taste
- 2 cups Greek yogurt

Directions:
1. In a food processor, blend cilantro, basil, garlic, walnuts, yogurt, salt, pepper, and half of the oil until smooth.
2. Warm the remaining oil in a skillet over medium heat. Brown pork meat for 5 minutes. Pour sauce over meat and bring to a boil. Cook for another 15 minutes. Serve.

Nutrition:
- Info Per Serving: Calories: 280;Fat: 12g;Protein: 19g;-Carbs: 21g.

Slow Cook Lamb Shanks With Cannellini Beans Stew

Servings:12 | Cooking Time: 10 Hours 15 Minutes

Ingredients:
- 1 can cannellini beans, rinsed and drained
- 1 large yellow onion, chopped
- 2 medium-sized carrots, diced
- 1 large stalk celery, chopped
- 2 cloves garlic, thinly sliced
- 4 lamb shanks, fat trimmed
- 2 teaspoons tarragon
- ½ teaspoon sea salt
- ¼ teaspoon ground black pepper
- 1 can diced tomatoes, with the juice

Directions:
1. Combine the beans, onion, carrots, celery, and garlic in the slow cooker. Stir to mix well.
2. Add the lamb shanks and sprinkle with tarragon, salt, and ground black pepper.
3. Pour in the tomatoes with juice, then cover the lid and cook on high for an hour.
4. Reduce the heat to low and cook for 9 hours or until the lamb is super tender.
5. Transfer the lamb on a plate, then pour the bean mixture in a colander over a separate bowl to reserve the liquid.
6. Let the liquid sit for 5 minutes until set, then skim the fat from the surface of the liquid. Pour the bean mixture back to the liquid.
7. Remove the bones from the lamb heat and discard the bones. Put the lamb meat and bean mixture back to the

slow cooker. Cover and cook to reheat for 15 minutes or until heated through.
8. Pour them on a large serving plate and serve immediately.

Nutrition:
- Info Per Serving: Calories: 317;Fat: 9.7g;Protein: 52.1g;-Carbs: 7.0g.

Citrusy Leg Lamb

Servings:4 | Cooking Time:7 Hours 10 Minutes

Ingredients:
- 2 cups stewed tomatoes, drained
- 3 ½ lb leg of lamb, cubed
- 1 lb small potatoes, cubed
- 1 grapefruit, zested and juiced
- 4 garlic cloves, minced
- Salt and black pepper to taste
- ½ cup basil, chopped

Directions:
1. Place potatoes, tomatoes, grapefruit juice, grapefruit zest, garlic, leg of lamb, salt, and pepper in your slow cooker. Cover with lid and cook for 8 hours on Low. Top with basil.

Nutrition:
- Info Per Serving: Calories: 300;Fat: 10g;Protein: 19g;-Carbs: 16g.

 Sweet Pork Stew

Servings:4 | Cooking Time:50 Minutes

Ingredients:
- 3 tbsp olive oil
- 1 ½ lb pork stew meat, cubed
- Salt and black pepper to taste
- 1 cup red onions, chopped
- 1 cup dried apricots, chopped
- 2 garlic cloves, minced
- 1 cup canned tomatoes, diced
- 2 tbsp parsley, chopped

Directions:
1. Warm olive oil in a skillet over medium heat. Sear pork meat for 5 minutes. Put in onions and cook for another 5 minutes. Stir in salt, pepper, apricots, garlic, tomatoes, and parsley and bring to a simmer and cook for an additional 30 minutes.

Nutrition:
- Info Per Serving: Calories: 320;Fat: 17g;Protein: 35g;-Carbs: 22g.

Baked Garlicky Pork Chops

Servings:4 | Cooking Time:45 Minutes

Ingredients:
- 1 tbsp olive oil
- 4 pork loin chops, boneless
- Salt and black pepper to taste
- 4 garlic cloves, minced
- 1 tbsp thyme, chopped

Directions:
1. Preheat the oven to 390° F. Place pork chops, salt, pepper, garlic, thyme, and olive oil in a roasting pan and bake for 10 minutes. Decrease the heat to 360° F and bake for 25 minutes.

Nutrition:
- Info Per Serving: Calories: 170;Fat: 6g;Protein: 26g;-Carbs: 2g.

Chicken Meatballs With Peach Topping

Servings:4 | Cooking Time:25 Minutes

Ingredients:
- 2 tbsp olive oil
- 1 lb ground chicken
- 2 peaches, cubed
- ½ red onion, finely chopped
- 1 lemon, juiced
- 1 garlic clove, minced
- ½ jalapeño pepper, minced
- 2 tbsp chopped fresh cilantro
- Salt and black pepper to taste

Directions:
1. Season the ground chicken with salt and pepper. Shape the mixture into meatballs. Warm olive oil in a pan over medium heat and brown fry the meatballs for 8-10 minutes on all sides until golden brown. In a bowl, combine peaches, lemon juice, garlic, red onion, jalapeño pepper, cilantro, and salt. Top the meatballs with the salsa and serve.

Nutrition:
- Info Per Serving: Calories: 312;Fat: 16g;Protein: 33.7g;-Carbs: 8g.

Aromatic Beef Stew

Servings:4 | Cooking Time:80 Minutes

Ingredients:
- 3 tbsp olive oil
- 2 lb beef shoulder, cubed
- Salt and black pepper to taste
- 1 onion, chopped
- 2 garlic cloves, minced
- 3 tomatoes, grated
- 1 tsp red chili flakes
- 2 cups chicken stock
- 1 cup couscous
- 10 green olives, sliced
- 1 tbsp cilantro, chopped

Directions:
1. Warm the olive oil in a pot over medium heat and cook beef for 5 minutes until brown, stirring often. Add in onion and garlic and cook for another 5 minutes. Stir in tomatoes, salt, pepper, chicken stock, olives, and red chili flakes. Bring to a boil and simmer for 1 hour. Cover the couscous with boiling water in a bowl, cover, and let sit for 4-5 minutes until the water has been absorbed. Fluff with a fork and season with salt and pepper. Pour the stew over and scatter with cilantro.

Nutrition:
- Info Per Serving: Calories: 420;Fat: 18g;Protein: 35g;-Carbs: 26g.

Saucy Green Pea & Chicken

Servings:4 | Cooking Time:40 Minutes

Ingredients:
- 2 tbsp olive oil
- 1 tsp dried thyme
- 1 lb chicken breasts, cubed
- Salt and black pepper to taste
- 1 cup chicken stock
- ½ cup tomato sauce
- 1 cup green peas
- 2 tbsp chives, chopped

Directions:
1. Warm the olive oil in a pot over medium heat and sauté the chicken for 8 minutes, stirring occasionally. Season with thyme, salt, and pepper. Pour in chicken stock and tomato sauce and bring to a boil. Simmer for 20 minutes. Add in green peas and cook for 4-5 minutes. Top with chives.

Nutrition:
- Info Per Serving: Calories: 316;Fat: 16g;Protein: 35g;-Carbs: 7g.

Milky Pork Stew

Servings:4 | Cooking Time:50 Minutes

Ingredients:
- 1 tbsp avocado oil
- 1 ½ cups buttermilk
- 1 ½ lb pork meat, cubed
- 1 red onion, chopped
- 1 garlic clove, minced
- ½ cup chicken stock
- 2 tbsp hot paprika
- Salt and black pepper to taste
- 1 tbsp cilantro, chopped

Directions:
1. Warm the avocado oil in a pot over medium heat and sear pork for 5 minutes. Put in onion and garlic and cook for 5 minutes. Stir in stock, paprika, salt, pepper, and buttermilk and bring to a boil; cook for 30 minutes. Top with cilantro.

Nutrition:
- Info Per Serving: Calories: 310;Fat: 10g;Protein: 23g;-Carbs: 16g.

Tuscan Pork Cassoulet

Servings:4 | Cooking Time:30 Minutes

Ingredients:
- 2 tbsp olive oil
- 2 lb pork loin, sliced
- 4 garlic cloves, minced
- 1 cup green olives, halved
- 1 tbsp capers
- ½ cup tomato puree
- Salt and black pepper to taste
- 2 tbsp parsley, chopped
- Juice of 1 lime

Directions:
1. Warm the olive oil in a skillet over medium heat and cook garlic and pork for 5 minutes. Stir in green olives, capers, tomato purée, salt, pepper, parsley, and lime juice and bring to a simmer. Cook for another 15 minutes. Serve.

Nutrition:
- Info Per Serving: Calories: 260;Fat: 13g;Protein: 14g;-Carbs: 22g.

Greek Wraps

Servings:2 | Cooking Time:10 Minutes

Ingredients:
- 2 cooked chicken breasts, shredded
- 2 tbsp roasted peppers, chopped
- 1 cup baby kale
- 2 whole-wheat tortillas
- 2 oz provolone cheese, grated
- 1 tomato, chopped
- 10 Kalamata olives, sliced
- 1 red onion, chopped

Directions:
1. In a bowl, mix all the ingredients except for the tortillas. Distribute the mixture across the tortillas and wrap them.

Nutrition:
- Info Per Serving: Calories: 200;Fat: 8g;Protein: 7g;-Carbs: 16g.

Beef Cherry & Tomato Cassoulet

Servings:4 | Cooking Time:30 Minutes

Ingredients:
- 3 tbsp olive oil
- 2 garlic cloves, minced
- 1 lemon, juiced and zested
- 1 ½ lb ground beef
- Salt and black pepper to taste
- 1 lb cherry tomatoes, halved
- 1 red onion, chopped
- 2 tbsp tomato paste
- 1 tbsp mint leaves, chopped

Directions:
1. Warm the olive oil in a skillet over medium heat and cook beef and garlic for 5 minutes. Stir in lemon zest, lemon juice, salt, pepper, cherry tomatoes, onion, tomato paste, and mint and cook for 15 minutes. Serve right away.

Nutrition:
- Info Per Serving: Calories: 324;Fat: 10g;Protein: 16g;-Carbs: 22g.

Greek-Style Veggie & Beef In Pita

Servings:2 | Cooking Time:30 Minutes

Ingredients:
- Beef
- 1 tbsp olive oil
- ½ medium onion, minced
- 2 garlic cloves, minced
- 6 oz lean ground beef
- 1 tsp dried oregano
- Yogurt Sauce
- ⅓ cup plain Greek yogurt
- 1 oz crumbled feta cheese
- 1 tbsp minced fresh dill
- 1 tbsp minced scallions
- 1 tbsp lemon juice
- Garlic salt to taste
- Sandwiches
- 2 Greek-style pitas, warm
- 6 cherry tomatoes, halved
- 1 cucumber, sliced
- Salt and black pepper to taste

Directions:

1. Warm the 1 tbsp olive oil in a pan over medium heat. Sauté the onion, garlic, and ground for 5-7 minutes, breaking up the meat well. When the meat is no longer pink, drain off any fat and stir in oregano. Turn off the heat.

2. In a small bowl, combine the yogurt, feta, dill, scallions, lemon juice, and garlic salt. Divide the yogurt sauce between the warm pitas. Top with ground beef, cherry tomatoes, and diced cucumber. Season with salt and pepper. Serve.

Nutrition:
- Info Per Serving: Calories: 541;Fat: 21g;Protein: 29g;-Carbs: 57g.

Simple Chicken With Olive Tapenade

Servings:4 | Cooking Time:35 Minutes

Ingredients:
- ½ cup olive oil
- 2 tbsp capers, canned
- 2 chicken breasts
- 1 cup black olives, pitted
- Salt and black pepper to taste
- ½ cup parsley, chopped
- ½ cup rosemary, chopped
- Salt and black pepper to taste
- 2 garlic cloves, minced
- ½ lemon, juiced and zested

Directions:

1. In a food processor, blend olives, capers, half of the oil, salt, pepper, parsley, rosemary, garlic, lemon zest, and lem-

on juice until smooth; set aside. Warm the remaining oil in a skillet over medium heat. Brown the chicken for 8-10 minutes on both sides. Top with tapenade. Serve and enjoy!

Nutrition:
- Info Per Serving: Calories: 300;Fat: 14g;Protein: 35g;-Carbs: 17g.

Pork Tenderloin With Caraway Seeds

Servings:4 | Cooking Time:30 Minutes

Ingredients:
- 2 tbsp olive oil
- 1 lb pork tenderloin, sliced
- Salt and black pepper to taste
- 3 tbsp ground caraway seeds
- 1/3 cup half-and-half
- ½ cup dill, chopped

Directions:

1. Warm the olive oil in a skillet over medium heat and sear pork for 8 minutes on all sides. Stir in salt, pepper, ground caraway seeds, half-and-half, and dill and bring to a boil. Cook for another 12 minutes. Serve warm.

Nutrition:
- Info Per Serving: Calories: 330;Fat: 15g;Protein: 18g;-Carbs: 15g.

Crispy Pork Chops

Servings:6 | Cooking Time:20 Minutes

Ingredients:
- 2 tbsp butter
- 3 tbsp olive oil
- 6 pork chops, boneless
- 2 fresh eggs
- 2 tbsp chicken stock
- ½ cup grated Parmesan cheese
- 1 cup panko bread crumbs
- 1 tsp Italian seasoning
- ½ tsp dried basil

Directions:

1. Flatten the chops with a meat tenderizer. In a bowl, beat the eggs with chicken stock. Mix the Parmesan cheese, crumbs, Italian seasoning, and basil on a shallow plate. Dip each pork chop into the egg mixture, then coat with the cheese mixture. Warm the butter and olive oil in a large skillet over medium heat. Sear the pork chops for 6-8 minutes on both sides until brown and crisp. Serve immediately.

Nutrition:
- Info Per Serving: Calories: 449;Fat: 22g;Protein: 46g;-Carbs: 15g.

Chicken Tagine With Vegetables

Servings:6 | Cooking Time:67 Minutes

Ingredients:
- 1 ½ lb boneless skinless chicken thighs, cut into chunks
- 2 zucchini, sliced into half-moons
- 4 tbsp olive oil
- Salt and black pepper to taste
- 1 small red onion, chopped
- 2 cloves garlic, minced
- 1 red bell pepper, chopped
- 2 tomatoes, chopped
- 1 tbsp harissa paste
- 1 cup water
- 1 cup black olives, halved
- ¼ cup fresh cilantro, chopped

Directions:
1. Warm the olive oil in a large skillet over medium heat. Season the chicken with salt and pepper and brown for 6-8 minutes on all sides. Add the onion, garlic, and bell pepper and sauté for 5 minutes until tender. Stir in harissa paste and tomatoes for 1 minute and pour in 1 cup of water. Bring to a boil and lower the heat to low. Cover and simmer for 35-45 minutes until the chicken is tender and cooked through. Stir in zucchini and olives and continue to cook for 10 minutes until the zucchini is tender. Serve topped with cilantro.

Nutrition:
- Info Per Serving: Calories: 358;Fat: 25g;Protein: 25g;-Carbs: 8g.

Chicken Bake With Cottage Cheese

Servings:4 | Cooking Time:40 Minutes

Ingredients:
- ¼ cup cottage cheese, crumbled
- 2 tbsp olive oil
- 1 lb chicken breasts, sliced
- 2 garlic cloves, minced
- ½ tsp onion powder
- Salt and black pepper to taste
- 4 red onions, sliced
- ¼ tsp dried oregano

Directions:
1. Preheat the oven to 360° F. Toss chicken, olive oil, garlic, dried oregano, onion powder, salt, pepper, and onions in a roasting pan and bake for 30 minutes. Top with cottage cheese.

Nutrition:
- Info Per Serving: Calories: 290;Fat: 16g;Protein: 25g;-Carbs: 16g.

Fish And Seafood

Fish And Seafood

Shrimp Quinoa Bowl With Black Olives

Servings:4 | Cooking Time:20 Minutes

Ingredients:
- 10 black olives, pitted and halved
- ¼ cup olive oil
- 1 cup quinoa
- 1 lemon, cut in wedges
- 1 lb shrimp, peeled and cooked
- 2 tomatoes, sliced
- 2 bell peppers, thinly sliced
- 1 red onion, chopped
- 1 tsp dried dill
- 1 tbsp fresh parsley, chopped
- Salt and black pepper to taste

Directions:
1. Place the quinoa in a pot and cover with 2 cups of water over medium heat. Bring to a boil, reduce the heat, and simmer for 12-15 minutes or until tender. Remove from heat and fluff it with a fork. Mix in the quinoa with olive oil, dill, parsley, salt, and black pepper. Stir in tomatoes, bell peppers, olives, and onion. Serve decorated with shrimp and lemon wedges.

Nutrition:
- Info Per Serving: Calories: 662;Fat: 21g;Protein: 79g;-Carbs: 38g.

Pan-fried Chili Sea Scallops

Servings:4 | Cooking Time:25 Minutes

Ingredients:
- 1 ½ lb large sea scallops, tendons removed
- 3 tbsp olive oil
- 1 garlic clove, finely chopped
- ½ red pepper flakes
- 2 tbsp chili sauce
- ¼ cup tomato sauce
- 1 small shallot, minced
- 1 tbsp minced fresh cilantro
- Salt and black pepper to taste

Directions:
1. Warm the olive oil in a skillet over medium heat. Add the scallops and cook for 2 minutes without moving them. Flip them and continue to cook for 2 more minutes, without moving them, until golden browned. Set aside. Add the shallot and garlic to the skillet and sauté for 3-5 minutes until softened. Pour in the chili sauce, tomato sauce, and red pepper flakes and stir for 3-4 minutes. Add the scal-

lops back and warm through. Adjust the taste and top with cilantro.

Nutrition:
- Info Per Serving: Calories: 204;Fat: 14.1g;Protein: 14g;-Carbs: 5g.

Spicy Grilled Shrimp With Lemon Wedges

Servings:6 | Cooking Time: 6 Minutes

Ingredients:
- 1 large clove garlic, crushed
- 1 teaspoon coarse salt
- 1 teaspoon paprika
- ½ teaspoon cayenne pepper
- 2 teaspoons lemon juice
- 2 tablespoons plus 1 teaspoon olive oil, divided
- 2 pounds large shrimp, peeled and deveined
- 8 wedges lemon, for garnish

Directions:
1. Preheat the grill to medium heat.
2. Stir together the garlic, salt, paprika, cayenne pepper, lemon juice, and 2 tablespoons of olive oil in a small bowl until a paste forms. Add the shrimp and toss until well coated.
3. Grease the grill grates lightly with remaining 1 teaspoon of olive oil.
4. Grill the shrimp for 4 to 6 minutes, flipping the shrimp halfway through, or until the shrimp is totally pink and opaque.
5. Garnish the shrimp with lemon wedges and serve hot.

Nutrition:
- Info Per Serving: Calories: 163;Fat: 5.8g;Protein: 25.2g;-Carbs: 2.8g.

Hake Fillet In Herby Tomato Sauce

Servings:4 | Cooking Time:30 Minutes

Ingredients:
- 2 tbsp olive oil
- 1 onion, sliced thin
- 1 fennel bulb, sliced
- Salt and black pepper to taste
- 4 garlic cloves, minced
- 1 tsp fresh thyme, chopped
- 1 can diced tomatoes,
- ½ cup dry white wine

- 4 skinless hake fillets
- 2 tbsp fresh basil, chopped

Directions:

1. Warm the olive oil in a skillet over medium heat. Sauté the onion and fennel for about 5 minutes until softened. Stir in garlic and thyme and cook for about 30 seconds until fragrant. Pour in tomatoes and wine and bring to simmer.

2. Season the hake with salt and pepper. Nestle hake skinned side down into the tomato sauce and spoon some sauce over the top. Bring to simmer. Cook for 10-12 minutes until hake easily flakes with a fork. Sprinkle with basil and serve.

Nutrition:

- Info Per Serving: Calories: 452;Fat: 9.9g;Protein: 78g;-Carbs: 9.7g.

Crispy Sole Fillets

Servings:4 | Cooking Time:10 Minutes

Ingredients:

- ¼ cup olive oil
- ½ cup flour
- ½ tsp paprika
- 8 skinless sole fillets
- Salt and black pepper to taste
- 4 lemon wedges

Directions:

1. Warm the olive oil in a skillet over medium heat. Mix the flour with paprika in a shallow dish. Coat the fish with the flour, shaking off any excess. Sear the sole fillets for 2-3 minutes per side until lightly browned. Serve with lemon wedges.

Nutrition:

- Info Per Serving: Calories: 219;Fat: 15g;Protein: 8.7g;-Carbs: 13g.

Roasted Red Snapper With Citrus Topping

Servings:2 | Cooking Time:35 Minutes

Ingredients:

- 2 tbsp olive oil
- 1 tsp fresh cilantro, chopped
- ½ tsp grated lemon zest
- ½ tbsp lemon juice
- ½ tsp grated grapefruit zest
- ½ tbsp grapefruit juice
- ½ tsp grated orange zest
- ½ tbsp orange juice
- ½ shallot, minced
- ¼ tsp red pepper flakes
- Salt and black pepper to taste
- 1 whole red snapper, cleaned

Directions:

1. Preheat oven to 380°F. Whisk the olive oil, cilantro, lemon juice, orange juice, grapefruit juice, shallot, and pepper flakes together in a bowl. Season with salt and pepper. Set aside the citrus topping until ready to serve.

2. In a separate bowl, combine lemon zest, orange zest, grapefruit zest, salt, and pepper. With a sharp knife, make 3-4 shallow slashes, about 2 inches apart, on both sides of the snapper. Spoon the citrus mixture into the fish cavity and transfer to a greased baking sheet. Roast for 25 minutes until the fish flakes. Serve drizzled with citrus topping, and enjoy!

Nutrition:

- Info Per Serving: Calories: 257;Fat: 21g;Protein: 16g;-Carbs: 1.6g.

Bell Pepper & Scallop Skillet

Servings:4 | Cooking Time:25 Minutes

Ingredients:

- 3 tbsp olive oil
- 2 celery stalks, sliced
- 2 lb sea scallops, halved
- 3 garlic cloves, minced
- Juice of 1 lime
- 1 red bell pepper, chopped
- 1 tbsp capers, chopped
- 1 tbsp mayonnaise
- 1 tbsp rosemary, chopped
- 1 cup chicken stock

Directions:

1. Warm olive oil in a skillet over medium heat and cook celery and garlic for 2 minutes. Stir in bell pepper, lime juice, capers, rosemary, and stock and bring to a boil. Simmer for 8 minutes. Mix in scallops and mayonnaise and cook for 5 minutes.

Nutrition:

- Info Per Serving: Calories: 310;Fat: 16g;Protein: 9g;-Carbs: 33g.

Crispy Herb Crusted Halibut

Servings:4 | Cooking Time: 20 Minutes

Ingredients:
- 4 halibut fillets, patted dry
- Extra-virgin olive oil, for brushing
- ½ cup coarsely ground unsalted pistachios
- 1 tablespoon chopped fresh parsley
- 1 teaspoon chopped fresh basil
- 1 teaspoon chopped fresh thyme
- Pinch sea salt
- Pinch freshly ground black pepper

Directions:
1. Preheat the oven to 350ºF. Line a baking sheet with parchment paper.
2. Place the fillets on the baking sheet and brush them generously with olive oil.
3. In a small bowl, stir together the pistachios, parsley, basil, thyme, salt, and pepper.
4. Spoon the nut mixture evenly on the fish, spreading it out so the tops of the fillets are covered.
5. Bake in the preheated oven until it flakes when pressed with a fork, about 20 minutes.
6. Serve immediately.

Nutrition:
- Info Per Serving: Calories: 262;Fat: 11.0g;Protein: 32.0g;Carbs: 4.0g.

Lemon Rosemary Roasted Branzino

Servings:2 | Cooking Time: 30 Minutes

Ingredients:
- 4 tablespoons extra-virgin olive oil, divided
- 2 branzino fillets, preferably at least 1 inch thick
- 1 garlic clove, minced
- 1 bunch scallions (white part only), thinly sliced
- 10 to 12 small cherry tomatoes, halved
- 1 large carrot, cut into ¼-inch rounds
- ½ cup dry white wine
- 2 tablespoons paprika
- 2 teaspoons kosher salt
- ½ tablespoon ground chili pepper
- 2 rosemary sprigs or 1 tablespoon dried rosemary
- 1 small lemon, thinly sliced
- ½ cup sliced pitted kalamata olives

Directions:
1. Heat a large ovenproof skillet over high heat until hot, about 2 minutes. Add 1 tablespoon of olive oil and heat for 10 to 15 seconds until it shimmers.
2. Add the branzino fillets, skin-side up, and sear for 2 minutes. Flip the fillets and cook for an additional 2 minutes. Set aside.
3. Swirl 2 tablespoons of olive oil around the skillet to

coat evenly.
4. Add the garlic, scallions, tomatoes, and carrot, and sauté for 5 minutes, or until softened.
5. Add the wine, stirring until all ingredients are well combined. Carefully place the fish over the sauce.
6. Preheat the oven to 450ºF.
7. Brush the fillets with the remaining 1 tablespoon of olive oil and season with paprika, salt, and chili pepper. Top each fillet with a rosemary sprig and lemon slices. Scatter the olives over fish and around the skillet.
8. Roast for about 10 minutes until the lemon slices are browned. Serve hot.

Nutrition:
- Info Per Serving: Calories: 724;Fat: 43.0g;Protein: 57.7g;Carbs: 25.0g.

Tuna Gyros With Tzatziki

Servings:4 | Cooking Time:15 Minutes

Ingredients:
- 4 oz tzatziki
- ½ lb canned tuna, drained
- ½ cup tahini
- 4 sundried tomatoes, diced
- 2 tbsp warm water
- 2 garlic cloves, minced
- 1 tbsp lemon juice
- 4 pita wraps
- 5 black olives, chopped
- Salt and black pepper to taste

Directions:
1. In a bowl, combine the tahini, water, garlic, lemon juice, salt, and black pepper. Warm the pita wraps in a grilled pan for a few minutes, turning once. Spread the tahini and tzatziki sauces over the warmed pitas and top with tuna, sundried tomatoes, and olives. Fold in half and serve immediately.

Nutrition:
- Info Per Serving: Calories: 334;Fat: 24g;Protein: 21.3g;-Carbs: 9g.

Lemony Shrimp With Orzo Salad

Servings:4 | Cooking Time: 22 Minutes

Ingredients:

- 1 cup orzo
- 1 hothouse cucumber, deseeded and chopped
- ½ cup finely diced red onion
- 2 tablespoons extra-virgin olive oil
- 2 pounds shrimp, peeled and deveined
- 3 lemons, juiced
- Salt and freshly ground black pepper, to taste
- ¾ cup crumbled feta cheese
- 2 tablespoons dried dill
- 1 cup chopped fresh flat-leaf parsley

Directions:

1. Bring a large pot of water to a boil. Add the orzo and cook covered for 15 to 18 minutes, or until the orzo is tender. Transfer to a colander to drain and set aside to cool.
2. Mix the cucumber and red onion in a bowl. Set aside.
3. Heat the olive oil in a medium skillet over medium heat until it shimmers.
4. Reduce the heat, add the shrimp, and cook each side for 2 minutes until cooked through.
5. Add the cooked shrimp to the bowl of cucumber and red onion. Mix in the cooked orzo and lemon juice and toss to combine. Sprinkle with salt and pepper. Scatter the top with the feta cheese and dill. Garnish with the parsley and serve immediately.

Nutrition:

- Info Per Serving: Calories: 565;Fat: 17.8g;Protein: 63.3g;Carbs: 43.9g.

Seafood Stew

Servings:4 | Cooking Time:25 Minutes

Ingredients:

- ½ lb skinless trout, cubed
- 2 tbsp olive oil
- ½ lb clams
- ½ lb cod, cubed
- 1 onion, chopped
- ½ fennel bulb, chopped
- 2 garlic cloves, minced
- ¼ cup dry white wine
- 2 tbsp chopped fresh parsley
- 1 can tomato sauce
- 1 cup fish broth
- 1 tbsp Italian seasoning
- ⅛ tsp red pepper flakes
- Salt and black pepper to taste

Directions:

1. Warm olive oil in a pot over medium heat and sauté onion and fennel for 5 minutes. Add in garlic and cook for

30 seconds. Pour in the wine and cook for 1 minute. Stir in tomato sauce, clams, broth, cod, trout, salt, Italian seasoning, red pepper flakes, and pepper. Bring just a boil and simmer for 5 minutes. Discard any unopened clams. Top with parsley.

Nutrition:

- Info Per Serving: Calories: 372;Fat: 15g;Protein: 34g;-Carbs: 25g.

Veggie & Clam Stew With Chickpeas

Servings:4 | Cooking Time:40 Minutes

Ingredients:

- 2 tbsp olive oil
- 1 yellow onion, chopped
- 1 fennel bulb, chopped
- 1 carrot, chopped
- 1 red bell pepper, chopped
- 2 garlic cloves, minced
- 3 tbsp tomato paste
- 16 oz canned chickpeas, drained
- 1 tsp dried thyme
- ¼ tsp smoked paprika
- Salt and black pepper to taste
- 1 lb clams, scrubbed

Directions:

1. Warm olive oil in a pot over medium heat and sauté fennel, onion, bell pepper, and carrot for 5 minutes until they're tender. Stir in garlic and tomato paste and cook for another minute. Mix in the chickpeas, thyme, paprika, salt, pepper, and 2 cups of water and bring to a boil; cook for 20 minutes.
2. Rinse the clams under cold, running water. Discard any clams that remain open when tapped with your fingers. Put the unopened clams into the pot and cook everything for 4-5 minutes until the shells have opened. When finished, discard any clams that haven't opened fully during the cooking process. Adjust the seasoning with salt and pepper. Serve.

Nutrition:

- Info Per Serving: Calories: 460;Fat: 13g;Protein: 35g;-Carbs: 48g.

Baked Fish With Pistachio Crust

Servings:4 | Cooking Time: 15 To 20 Minutes

Ingredients:
- ½ cup extra-virgin olive oil, divided
- 1 pound flaky white fish (such as cod, haddock, or halibut), skin removed
- ½ cup shelled finely chopped pistachios
- ½ cup ground flaxseed
- Zest and juice of 1 lemon, divided
- 1 teaspoon ground cumin
- 1 teaspoon ground allspice
- ½ teaspoon salt
- ¼ teaspoon freshly ground black pepper

Directions:
1. Preheat the oven to 400°F.
2. Line a baking sheet with parchment paper or aluminum foil and drizzle 2 tablespoons of olive oil over the sheet, spreading to evenly coat the bottom.
3. Cut the fish into 4 equal pieces and place on the prepared baking sheet.
4. In a small bowl, combine the pistachios, flaxseed, lemon zest, cumin, allspice, salt, and pepper. Drizzle in ¼ cup of olive oil and stir well.
5. Divide the nut mixture evenly on top of the fish pieces. Drizzle the lemon juice and remaining 2 tablespoons of olive oil over the fish and bake until cooked through, 15 to 20 minutes, depending on the thickness of the fish.
6. Cool for 5 minutes before serving.

Nutrition:
- Info Per Serving: Calories: 509;Fat: 41.0g;Protein: 26.0g;Carbs: 9.0g.

One-Skillet Salmon With Olives & Escarole

Servings:4 | Cooking Time:25 Minutes

Ingredients:
- 3 tbsp olive oil
- 1 head escarole, torn
- 4 salmon fillets, boneless
- 1 lime, juiced
- Salt and black pepper to taste
- ¼ cup fish stock
- ¼ cup green olives, pitted and chopped
- ¼ cup fresh chives, chopped

Directions:
1. Warm half of the olive oil in a skillet over medium heat and sauté escarole, lime juice, salt, pepper, fish stock, and olives for 6 minutes. Share into plates. Warm the remaining oil in the same skillet. Sprinkle salmon with salt and pepper and fry for 8 minutes on both sides until golden brown. Transfer to the escarole plates and serve warm topped with chives.

Nutrition:
- Info Per Serving: Calories: 280;Fat: 15g;Protein: 19g;-Carbs: 25g.

Spiced Flounder With Pasta Salad

Servings:4 | Cooking Time:25 Minutes

Ingredients:
- 2 tbsp olive oil
- 4 flounder fillets, boneless
- 1 tsp rosemary, dried
- 2 tsp cumin, ground
- 1 tbsp coriander, ground
- 2 tsp cinnamon powder
- 2 tsp oregano, dried
- Salt and black pepper to taste
- 2 cups macaroni, cooked
- 1 cup cherry tomatoes, halved
- 1 avocado, peeled and sliced
- 1 cucumber, cubed
- ½ cup black olives, sliced
- 1 lemon, juiced

Directions:
1. Preheat the oven to 390 °F. Combine rosemary, cumin, coriander, cinnamon, oregano, salt, and pepper in a bowl. Add in the flounder and toss to coat.
2. Warm olive oil in a skillet over medium heat. Brown the fish fillets for 4 minutes on both sides. Transfer to a baking tray and bake in the oven for 7-10 minutes. Combine macaroni, tomatoes, avocado, cucumber, olives, and lemon juice in a bowl; toss to coat. Serve the fish with pasta salad on the side.

Nutrition:
- Info Per Serving: Calories: 370;Fat: 16g;Protein: 26g;-Carbs: 57g.

Hot Tomato & Caper Squid Stew

Servings:4 | Cooking Time:50 Minutes

Ingredients:
- 1 cans whole peeled tomatoes, diced
- ¼ cup olive oil
- 1 onion, chopped
- 1 celery rib, sliced
- 3 garlic cloves, minced
- ¼ tsp red pepper flakes
- 1 red chili, minced
- ½ cup dry white wine
- 2 lb squid, sliced into rings
- Salt and black pepper to taste
- ⅓ cup green olives, chopped

- 1 tbsp capers
- 2 tbsp fresh parsley, chopped

Directions:

1. Warm the olive oil in a pot over medium heat. Sauté the onion, garlic, red chili, and celery until softened, about 5 minutes. Stir in pepper flakes and cook for about 30 seconds. Stir in wine, scraping up any browned bits, and cook until nearly evaporated, about 1 minute. Add 1 cup of water and season with salt and pepper. Stir the squid in the pot. Reduce heat to low, cover, and simmer until squid has released its liquid, about 15 minutes. Pour in tomatoes, olives, and capers, and continue to cook until squid is very tender, 30-35 minutes. Top with parsley. Serve and enjoy!

Nutrition:

- Info Per Serving: Calories: 334;Fat: 12g;Protein: 28g;-Carbs: 30g.

Roman-Style Cod

Servings:2 | Cooking Time:40 Minutes

Ingredients:

- 2 cod fillets, cut in 4 portions
- ¼ tsp paprika
- ¼ tsp onion powder
- 3 tbsp olive oil
- 4 medium scallions
- 2 tbsp fresh chopped basil
- 3 tbsp minced garlic
- Salt and black pepper to taste
- ¼ tsp dry marjoram
- 6 sun-dried tomato slices
- ½ cup dry white wine
- ½ cup ricotta cheese, crumbled
- 1 can artichoke hearts
- 1 lemon, sliced
- 1 cup pitted black olives
- 1 tsp capers

Directions:

1. Preheat oven to 375 °F. Warm the olive oil in a skillet over medium heat. Sprinkle the cod with paprika and onion powder. Sear it for about 1 minute per side or until golden; reserve. Add the scallions, basil, garlic, salt, pepper, marjoram, tomatoes, and wine to the same skillet. Bring to a boil. Remove the skillet from the heat. Arrange the fish on top of the sauce and sprinkle with ricotta cheese.

2. Place the artichokes in the pan and top with lemon slices. Sprinkle with black olives and capers. Place the skillet in the oven. Bake for 15-20 minutes until it flakes easily with a fork.

Nutrition:

- Info Per Serving: Calories: 1172;Fat: 59g;Protein: 64g;-Carbs: 94g.

Lemon Trout With Roasted Beets

Servings:4 | Cooking Time:45 Minutes

Ingredients:

- 1 lb medium beets, peeled and sliced
- 3 tbsp olive oil
- 4 trout fillets, boneless
- Salt and black pepper to taste
- 1 tbsp rosemary, chopped
- 2 spring onions, chopped
- 2 tbsp lemon juice
- ½ cup vegetable stock

Directions:

1. Preheat oven to 390°F. Line a baking sheet with parchment paper. Arrange the beets on the sheet, season with salt and pepper, and drizzle with some olive oil. Roast for 20 minutes.

2. Warm the remaining oil in a skillet over medium heat. Cook trout fillets for 8 minutes on all sides; reserve. Add spring onions to the skillet and sauté for 2 minutes. Stir in lemon juice and stock and cook for 5-6 minutes until the sauce thickens. Remove the beets to a plate and top with trout fillets. Pour the sauce all over and sprinkle with rosemary.

Nutrition:

- Info Per Serving: Calories: 240;Fat: 6g;Protein: 18g;-Carbs: 22g.

Crispy Salmon Patties With Grecian Sauce

Servings:2 | Cooking Time:30 Minutes

Ingredients:

- 1 cup tzatziki sauce
- 2 tsp olive oil
- Salmon cakes
- 6 oz cooked salmon, flaked
- ¼ cup celery, minced
- ¼ cup onion, minced
- ¼ tsp chili powder
- ½ tsp dried dill
- 1 tbsp fresh minced parsley
- Salt and black pepper to taste
- 1 egg, beaten
- ½ cup breadcrumbs

Directions:

1. In a large bowl, mix well all the salmon cake ingredients. Shape the mixture into balls, then press them to form patties.

2. Warm the olive oil in a skillet over medium heat. Cook the patties for 3 minutes per side or until they're golden brown. Serve the salmon cakes topped with the tzatziki sauce.

Nutrition:
• Info Per Serving: Calories: 555;Fat: 41g;Protein: 31g;-Carbs: 18g.

Mackerel And Green Bean Salad

Servings:2 | Cooking Time: 10 Minutes

Ingredients:
• 2 cups green beans
• 1 tablespoon avocado oil
• 2 mackerel fillets
• 4 cups mixed salad greens
• 2 hard-boiled eggs, sliced
• 1 avocado, sliced
• 2 tablespoons lemon juice
• 2 tablespoons olive oil
• 1 teaspoon Dijon mustard
• Salt and black pepper, to taste

Directions:
1. Cook the green beans in a medium saucepan of boiling water for about 3 minutes until crisp-tender. Drain and set aside.
2. Melt the avocado oil in a pan over medium heat. Add the mackerel fillets and cook each side for 4 minutes.
3. Divide the greens between two salad bowls. Top with the mackerel, sliced egg, and avocado slices.
4. In another bowl, whisk together the lemon juice, olive oil, mustard, salt, and pepper, and drizzle over the salad. Add the cooked green beans and toss to combine, then serve.

Nutrition:
• Info Per Serving: Calories: 737;Fat: 57.3g;Protein: 34.2g;Carbs: 22.1g.

Cod Fettuccine

Servings:4 | Cooking Time:30 Minutes

Ingredients:
• 1 lb cod fillets, cubed
• 16 oz fettuccine
• 3 tbsp olive oil
• 1 onion, finely chopped
• Salt and lemon pepper to taste
• 1 ½ cups heavy cream
• 1 cup Parmesan cheese, grated

Directions:
1. Boil salted water in a pot over medium heat and stir in fettuccine. Cook according to package directions and drain. Heat the olive oil in a large saucepan over medium heat and add the onion. Stir-fry for 3 minutes until tender. Sprinkle cod with salt and lemon pepper and add to saucepan; cook for 4–5 minutes until fish fillets and flakes easily

with a fork. Stir in heavy cream for 2 minutes. Add in the pasta, tossing gently to combine. Cook for 3–4 minutes until sauce is slightly thickened. Sprinkle with Parmesan cheese.

Nutrition:
• Info Per Serving: Calories: 431;Fat: 36g;Protein: 42g;-Carbs: 97g.

Fennel Poached Cod With Tomatoes

Servings:4 | Cooking Time: 20 Minutes

Ingredients:
• 1 tablespoon olive oil
• 1 cup thinly sliced fennel
• ½ cup thinly sliced onion
• 1 tablespoon minced garlic
• 1 can diced tomatoes
• 2 cups chicken broth
• ½ cup white wine
• Juice and zest of 1 orange
• 1 pinch red pepper flakes
• 1 bay leaf
• 1 pound cod

Directions:
1. Heat the olive oil in a large skillet. Add the onion and fennel and cook for 6 minutes, stirring occasionally, or until translucent. Add the garlic and cook for 1 minute more.
2. Add the tomatoes, chicken broth, wine, orange juice and zest, red pepper flakes, and bay leaf, and simmer for 5 minutes to meld the flavors.
3. Carefully add the cod in a single layer, cover, and simmer for 6 to 7 minutes.
4. Transfer fish to a serving dish, ladle the remaining sauce over the fish, and serve.

Nutrition:
• Info Per Serving: Calories: 336;Fat: 12.5g;Protein: 45.1g;Carbs: 11.0g.

Lemon Grilled Shrimp

Servings:4 | Cooking Time: 4 To 6 Minutes

Ingredients:
• 2 tablespoons garlic, minced
• 3 tablespoons fresh Italian parsley, finely chopped
• ¼ cup extra-virgin olive oil
• ½ cup lemon juice
• 1 teaspoon salt
• 2 pounds jumbo shrimp, peeled and deveined
• Special Equipment:
• 4 skewers, soaked in water for at least 30 minutes

Directions:
1. Whisk together the garlic, parsley, olive oil, lemon

juice, and salt in a large bowl.

2. Add the shrimp to the bowl and toss well, making sure the shrimp are coated in the marinade. Set aside to sit for 15 minutes.

3. When ready, skewer the shrimps by piercing through the center. You can place about 5 to 6 shrimps on each skewer.

4. Preheat the grill to high heat.

5. Grill the shrimp for 4 to 6 minutes, flipping the shrimp halfway through, or until the shrimp are pink on the outside and opaque in the center.

6. Serve hot.

Nutrition:
• Info Per Serving: Calories: 401;Fat: 17.8g;Protein: 56.9g;Carbs: 3.9g.

Trout Fillets With Horseradish Sauce

Servings:4 | Cooking Time:35 Minutes

Ingredients:
• 3 tbsp olive oil
• 2 tbsp horseradish sauce
• 1 onion, sliced
• 2 tsp Italian seasoning
• 4 trout fillets, boneless
• ¼ cup panko breadcrumbs
• ½ cup green olives, pitted and chopped
• Salt and black pepper to taste
• 1 lemon, juiced

Directions:
1. Preheat the oven to 380°F. Line a baking sheet with parchment paper. Sprinkle trout fillets with salt and pepper and dip in breadcrumbs. Arrange them along with the onion on the sheet. Sprinkle with olive oil, Italian seasoning, and lemon juice and bake for 15-18 minutes. Transfer to a serving plate and top with horseradish sauce and olives. Serve right away.

Nutrition:
• Info Per Serving: Calories: 310;Fat: 10g;Protein: 16g;-Carbs: 25g.

Walnut-Crusted Salmon

Servings:4 | Cooking Time:25 Minutes

Ingredients:
• 2 tbsp olive oil
• 4 salmon fillets, boneless
• 2 tbsp mustard
• 5 tsp honey
• 1 cup walnuts, chopped
• 1 tbsp lemon juice
• 2 tsp parsley, chopped
• Salt and pepper to the taste

Directions:
1. Preheat the oven to 380°F. Line a baking tray with parchment paper. In a bowl, whisk the olive oil, mustard, and honey. In a separate bowl, combine walnuts and parsley. Sprinkle salmon with salt and pepper and place them on the tray. Rub each fillet with mustard mixture and scatter with walnut mixture; bake for 15 minutes. Drizzle with lemon juice.

Nutrition:
• Info Per Serving: Calories: 300;Fat: 16g;Protein: 17g;-Carbs: 22g.

Halibut Confit With Sautéed Leeks

Servings:4 | Cooking Time:45 Minutes

Ingredients:
• 1 tsp fresh lemon zest
• ¼ cup olive oil
• 4 skinless halibut fillets
• Salt and black pepper to taste
• 1 lb leeks, sliced
• 1 tsp Dijon mustard
• ¾ cup dry white wine
• 1 tbsp fresh cilantro, chopped
• 4 lemon wedges

Directions:
1. Warm the olive oil in a skillet over medium heat. Season the halibut with salt and pepper. Sear in the skillet for 6-7 minutes until cooked all the way through. Carefully transfer the halibut to a large plate. Add leeks, mustard, salt, and pepper to the skillet and sauté for 10-12 minutes, stirring frequently, until softened. Pour in the wine and lemon zest and bring to a simmer. Top with halibut. Reduce the heat to low, cover, and simmer for 6-10 minutes. Carefully transfer halibut to a serving platter, tent loosely with aluminum foil, and let rest while finishing leeks. Increase the heat and cook the leeks for 2-4 minutes until the sauce is slightly thickened. Adjust the seasoning with salt and pepper. Pour the leek mixture around the halibut, sprinkle with cilantro, and serve with lemon wedges.

Nutrition:
• Info Per Serving: Calories: 566;Fat: 19g;Protein: 78g;-Carbs: 17g.

Creamy Halibut & Potato Soup

Servings:4 | Cooking Time:25 Minutes

Ingredients:
- 3 gold potatoes, peeled and cubed
- 4 oz halibut fillets, boneless and cubed
- 2 tbsp olive oil
- 2 carrots, chopped
- 1 red onion, chopped
- Salt and white pepper to taste
- 4 cups fish stock
- ½ cup heavy cream
- 1 tbsp dill, chopped

Directions:
1. Warm the olive oil in a skillet over medium heat and cook the onion for 3 minutes. Put in potatoes, salt, pepper, carrots, and stock and bring to a boil. Cook for an additional 5-6 minutes. Stir in halibut, cream, and dill and simmer for another 5 minutes. Serve right away.

Nutrition:
- Info Per Serving: Calories: 215;Fat: 17g;Protein: 12g;-Carbs: 7g.

Pancetta-Wrapped Scallops

Servings:6 | Cooking Time:25 Minutes

Ingredients:
- 2 tsp olive oil
- 12 thin pancetta slices
- 12 medium scallops
- 2 tsp lemon juice
- 1 tsp chili powder

Directions:
1. Wrap pancetta around scallops and secure with toothpicks. Warm the olive oil in a skillet over medium heat and cook scallops for 6 minutes on all sides. Serve sprinkled with chili powder and lemon juice.

Nutrition:
- Info Per Serving: Calories: 310;Fat: 25g;Protein: 19g;-Carbs: 24g.

Tuna And Zucchini Patties

Servings:4 | Cooking Time: 12 Minutes

Ingredients:
- 3 slices whole-wheat sandwich bread, toasted
- 2 cans tuna in olive oil, drained
- 1 cup shredded zucchini
- 1 large egg, lightly beaten
- ¼ cup diced red bell pepper
- 1 tablespoon dried oregano
- 1 teaspoon lemon zest
- ¼ teaspoon freshly ground black pepper
- ¼ teaspoon kosher or sea salt
- 1 tablespoon extra-virgin olive oil
- Salad greens or 4 whole-wheat rolls, for serving (optional)

Directions:
1. Crumble the toast into bread crumbs with your fingers (or use a knife to cut into ¼-inch cubes) until you have 1 cup of loosely packed crumbs. Pour the crumbs into a large bowl. Add the tuna, zucchini, beaten egg, bell pepper, oregano, lemon zest, black pepper, and salt. Mix well with a fork. With your hands, form the mixture into four (½-cup-size) patties. Place them on a plate, and press each patty flat to about ¾-inch thick.
2. In a large skillet over medium-high heat, heat the oil until it's very hot, about 2 minutes.
3. Add the patties to the hot oil, then reduce the heat down to medium. Cook the patties for 5 minutes, flip with a spatula, and cook for an additional 5 minutes. Serve the patties on salad greens or whole-wheat rolls, if desired.

Nutrition:
- Info Per Serving: Calories: 757;Fat: 72.0g;Protein: 5.0g;-Carbs: 26.0g.

Baked Haddock With Rosemary Gremolata

Servings:6 | Cooking Time:35 Min + Marinating Time

Ingredients:
- 1 cup milk
- Salt and black pepper to taste
- 2 tbsp rosemary, chopped
- 1 garlic clove, minced
- 1 lemon, zested
- 1 ½ lb haddock fillets

Directions:
1. In a large bowl, coat the fish with milk, salt, pepper, and 1 tablespoon of rosemary. Refrigerate for 2 hours.
2. Preheat oven to 380ºF. Carefully remove the haddock from the marinade, drain thoroughly, and place in a greased baking dish. Cover and bake 15–20 minutes until the fish is flaky. Remove fish from the oven and let it rest 5 minutes. To make the gremolata, mix the remaining rosemary, lemon zest, and garlic. Sprinkle the fish with gremolata and serve.

Nutrition:
- Info Per Serving: Calories: 112;Fat: 2g;Protein: 20g;-Carbs: 3g.

Lemony Trout With Caramelized Shallots

Servings:2 | Cooking Time: 20 Minutes

Ingredients:
- Shallots:
- 1 teaspoon almond butter
- 2 shallots, thinly sliced
- Dash salt
- Trout:
- 1 tablespoon plus 1 teaspoon almond butter, divided
- 2 trout fillets
- 3 tablespoons capers
- ¼ cup freshly squeezed lemon juice
- ¼ teaspoon salt
- Dash freshly ground black pepper
- 1 lemon, thinly sliced

Directions:
1. Make the Shallots
2. In a large skillet over medium heat, cook the butter, shallots, and salt for 20 minutes, stirring every 5 minutes, or until the shallots are wilted and caramelized.
3. Make the Trout
4. Meanwhile, in another large skillet over medium heat, heat 1 teaspoon of almond butter.
5. Add the trout fillets and cook each side for 3 minutes, or until flaky. Transfer to a plate and set aside.
6. In the skillet used for the trout, stir in the capers, lemon juice, salt, and pepper, then bring to a simmer. Whisk in the remaining 1 tablespoon of almond butter. Spoon the sauce over the fish.
7. Garnish the fish with the lemon slices and caramelized shallots before serving.

Nutrition:
- Info Per Serving: Calories: 344;Fat: 18.4g;Protein: 21.1g;Carbs: 14.7g.

Caper & Squid Stew

Servings:4 | Cooking Time:25 Minutes

Ingredients:
- 2 tbsp olive oil
- 1 onion, chopped
- 1 celery stalk, chopped
- 1 lb calamari rings
- 2 red chili peppers, chopped
- 2 garlic cloves, minced
- 14 oz canned tomatoes, diced
- 2 tbsp tomato paste
- Salt and black pepper to taste
- 2 tbsp capers, drained
- 12 black olives, pitted and halved

Directions:

1. Warm the olive oil in a skillet over medium heat and cook onion, celery, garlic, and chili peppers for 2 minutes. Stir in calamari rings, tomatoes, tomato paste, salt, and pepper and bring to a simmer. Cook for 20 minutes. Put in olives and capers and cook for another 5 minutes. Serve right away.

Nutrition:
- Info Per Serving: Calories: 280;Fat: 12g;Protein: 16g;-Carbs: 14g.

One-pot Shrimp With White Beans

Servings:4 | Cooking Time:23 Minutes

Ingredients:
- 1 lb large shrimp, peeled and deveined
- 3 tbsp olive oil
- Salt and black pepper to taste
- 1 red bell pepper, chopped
- 1 small red onion, chopped
- 2 garlic cloves, minced
- ¼ tsp red pepper flakes
- 2 cans cannellini beans
- 2 tbsp lemon zest

Directions:
1. Warm the olive oil in a skillet over medium heat. Add the shrimp and cook, without stirring, until spotty brown and edges turn pink, about 2 minutes. Remove the skillet from the heat, turn over the shrimp, and let sit until opaque throughout, about 30 seconds. Transfer shrimp to a bowl and cover with foil to keep warm.
2. Return the skillet to heat and reheat the olive oil. Sauté the bell pepper, garlic, and onion until softened, about 5 minutes. Stir in pepper flakes and salt for about 30 seconds. Pour in the beans and cook until heated through, 5 minutes. Add the shrimp with any accumulated juices back to the skillet cook for about 1 minute. Stir in lemon zest and serve.

Nutrition:
- Info Per Serving: Calories: 300;Fat: 18g;Protein: 25g;-Carbs: 11g.

Parchment Orange & Dill Salmon

Servings:4 | Cooking Time:25 Minutes

Ingredients:
- 2 tbsp butter, melted
- 4 salmon fillets
- Salt and black pepper to taste
- 1 orange, juiced and zested
- 4 tbsp fresh dill, chopped

Directions:

1. Preheat oven to 375 °F. Coat the salmon fillets on both sides with butter. Season with salt and pepper and divide them between 4 pieces of parchment paper. Drizzle the orange juice over each piece of fish and top with orange zest and dill. Wrap the paper around the fish to make packets. Place on a baking sheet and bake for 15-20 minutes until the cod is cooked through. Serve and enjoy!

Nutrition:
- Info Per Serving: Calories: 481;Fat: 21g;Protein: 65g;-Carbs: 4.2g.

Lemon-garlic Sea Bass

Servings:2 | Cooking Time:25 Minutes

Ingredients:
- 2 tbsp olive oil
- 2 sea bass fillets
- 1 lemon, juiced
- 4 garlic cloves, minced
- Salt and black pepper to taste

Directions:

1. Preheat the oven to 380°F. Line a baking sheet with parchment paper. Brush sea bass fillets with lemon juice, olive oil, garlic, salt, and pepper and arrange them on the sheet. Bake for 15 minutes. Serve with salad.

Nutrition:
- Info Per Serving: Calories: 530;Fat: 30g;Protein: 54g;-Carbs: 15g.

Hot Jumbo Shrimp

Servings:4 | Cooking Time:20 Minutes

Ingredients:
- 2 lb shell-on jumbo shrimp, deveined
- ¼ cup olive oil
- Salt and black pepper to taste
- 6 garlic cloves, minced
- 1 tsp anise seeds
- ½ tsp red pepper flakes
- 2 tbsp minced fresh cilantro
- 1 lemon, cut into wedges

Directions:

1. Combine the olive oil, garlic, anise seeds, pepper flakes, and black pepper in a large bowl. Add the shrimp and cilantro and toss well, making sure the oil mixture gets into the interior of the shrimp. Arrange shrimp in a single layer on a baking tray. Set under the preheated broiler for approximately 4 minutes. Flip shrimp and continue to broil until it is opaque and shells are beginning to brown, about 2 minutes, rotating sheet halfway through broiling. Serve with lemon wedges.

Nutrition:
- Info Per Serving: Calories: 218;Fat: 9g;Protein: 30.8g;-Carbs: 2.3g.

Vegetable & Shrimp Roast

Servings:4 | Cooking Time:30 Minutes

Ingredients:
- 2 lb shrimp, peeled and deveined
- 4 tbsp olive oil
- 2 bell peppers, cut into chunks
- 2 fennel bulbs, cut into wedges
- 2 red onions, cut into wedges
- 4 garlic cloves, unpeeled
- 8 Kalamata olives, halved
- 1 tsp lemon zest, grated
- 2 tsp oregano, dried
- 2 tbsp parsley, chopped
- Salt and black pepper to taste

Directions:

1. Preheat the oven to 390 °F. Place bell peppers, garlic, fennel, red onions, and olives in a roasting tray. Add in the lemon zest, oregano, half of the olive oil, salt, and pepper and toss to coat; roast for 15 minutes. Coat the shrimp with the remaining olive oil and pour over the veggies; roast for another 7 minutes. Serve topped with parsley.

Nutrition:
- Info Per Serving: Calories: 350;Fat: 20g;Protein: 11g;-Carbs: 35g.

Steamed Mussels With Spaghetti

Servings:4 | Cooking Time:30 Minutes

Ingredients:
- 2 lb mussels, cleaned and beards removed
- 1 lb cooked spaghetti
- 3 tbsp butter
- 2 garlic cloves, minced
- 1 carrot, diced
- 1 onion, chopped
- 2 celery sticks, chopped
- 1 cup white wine
- 2 tbsp parsley, chopped

- ½ tsp red pepper flakes
- 1 lemon, juiced

Directions:

1. Melt butter in a saucepan over medium heat and sauté the garlic, carrot, onion, and celery for 4-5 minutes, stirring occasionally until softened. Add the mussels, white wine, and lemon juice, cover, and bring to a boil. Reduce the heat and steam the for 4-6 minutes. Discard any unopened mussels. Stir in spaghetti to coat. Sprinkle with parsley and red pepper flakes to serve.

Nutrition:

- Info Per Serving: Calories: 669;Fat: 16g;Protein: 41g;- Carbs: 77g.

Mushroom & Shrimp Rice

Servings:4 | Cooking Time:40 Minutes

Ingredients:

- 2 tbsp olive oil
- 1 lb shrimp, peeled, deveined
- 1 cup white rice
- 4 garlic cloves, sliced
- ¼ tsp hot paprika
- 1 cup mushrooms, sliced
- ¼ cup green peas
- Juice of 1 lime
- Sea salt to taste
- ¼ cup chopped fresh chives

Directions:

1. Bring a pot of salted water to a boil. Cook the rice for 15-18 minutes, stirring occasionally. Drain and place in a bowl. Add in the green peas and mix to combine well. Taste and adjust the seasoning. Remove to a serving plate.
2. Heat the olive oil in a saucepan over medium heat and sauté garlic and hot paprika for 30-40 seconds until garlic is light golden brown. Remove the garlic with a slotted spoon. Add the mushrooms to the saucepan and sauté them for 5 minutes until tender. Put in the shrimp, lime juice, and salt and stir for 4 minutes. Turn the heat off. Add the chives and reserved garlic to the shrimp and pour over the rice. Serve and enjoy!

Nutrition:

- Info Per Serving: Calories: 342;Fat: 12g;Protein: 24g;- Carbs: 33g.

Vegetable Mains And Meatless

Vegetable Mains And Meatless

Baked Honey Acorn Squash

Servings:4 | Cooking Time:35 Minutes

Ingredients:
- 1 acorn squash, cut into wedges
- 2 tbsp olive oil
- 2 tbsp honey
- 2 tbsp rosemary, chopped
- 2 tbsp walnuts, chopped

Directions:
1. Preheat oven to 400°F. In a bowl, mix honey, rosemary, and olive oil. Lay the squash wedges on a baking sheet and drizzle with the honey mixture. Bake for 30 minutes until squash is tender and slightly caramelized, turning each slice over halfway through. Serve cooled sprinkled with walnuts.

Nutrition:
- Info Per Serving: Calories: 136;Fat: 6g;Protein: 0.9g;-Carbs: 20g.

Baked Beet & Leek With Dilly Yogurt

Servings:4 | Cooking Time:40 Minutes

Ingredients:
- 5 tbsp olive oil
- ½ lb leeks, thickly sliced
- 1 lb red beets, sliced
- 1 cup yogurt
- 2 garlic cloves, finely minced
- ¼ tsp cumin, ground
- ¼ tsp dried parsley
- ¼ cup parsley, chopped
- 1 tsp dill
- Salt and black pepper to taste

Directions:
1. Preheat the oven to 390°F. Arrange the beets and leeks on a greased roasting dish. Sprinkle with some olive oil, cumin, dried parsley, black pepper, and salt. Bake in the oven for 25-30 minutes. Transfer to a serving platter. In a bowl, stir in yogurt, dill, garlic, and the remaining olive oil. Whisk to combine. Drizzle the veggies with the yogurt sauce and top with fresh parsley to serve.

Nutrition:
- Info Per Serving: Calories: 281;Fat: 18.7g;Protein: 6g;-Carbs: 24g.

Stir-fried Kale With Mushrooms

Servings:4 | Cooking Time:10 Minutes

Ingredients:
- 1 cup cremini mushrooms, sliced
- 4 tbsp olive oil
- 1 small red onion, chopped
- 2 cloves garlic, thinly sliced
- 1 ½ lb curly kale
- 2 tomatoes, chopped
- 1 tsp dried oregano
- 1 tsp dried basil
- ½ tsp dried rosemary
- ½ tsp dried thyme
- Salt and black pepper to taste

Directions:
1. Warm the olive oil in a saucepan over medium heat. Sauté the onion and garlic for about 3 minutes or until they are softened. Add in the mushrooms, kale, and tomatoes, stirring to promote even cooking. Turn the heat to a simmer, add in the spices and cook for 5-6 minutes until the kale wilt.

Nutrition:
- Info Per Serving: Calories: 221;Fat: 16g;Protein: 9g;-Carbs: 19g.

Wilted Dandelion Greens With Sweet Onion

Servings:4 | Cooking Time: 15 Minutes

Ingredients:
- 1 tablespoon extra-virgin olive oil
- 2 garlic cloves, minced
- 1 Vidalia onion, thinly sliced
- ½ cup low-sodium vegetable broth
- 2 bunches dandelion greens, roughly chopped
- Freshly ground black pepper, to taste

Directions:
1. Heat the olive oil in a large skillet over low heat.
2. Add the garlic and onion and cook for 2 to 3 minutes, stirring occasionally, or until the onion is translucent.
3. Fold in the vegetable broth and dandelion greens and cook for 5 to 7 minutes until wilted, stirring frequently.
4. Sprinkle with the black pepper and serve on a plate while warm.

Nutrition:
- Info Per Serving: Calories: 81;Fat: 3.9g;Protein: 3.2g;-Carbs: 10.8g.

Garlicky Zucchini Cubes With Mint

Servings:4 | Cooking Time: 10 Minutes

Ingredients:
- 3 large green zucchinis, cut into ½-inch cubes
- 3 tablespoons extra-virgin olive oil
- 1 large onion, chopped
- 3 cloves garlic, minced
- 1 teaspoon salt
- 1 teaspoon dried mint

Directions:
1. Heat the olive oil in a large skillet over medium heat.
2. Add the onion and garlic and sauté for 3 minutes, stirring constantly, or until softened.
3. Stir in the zucchini cubes and salt and cook for 5 minutes, or until the zucchini is browned and tender.
4. Add the mint to the skillet and toss to combine, then continue cooking for 2 minutes.
5. Serve warm.

Nutrition:
- Info Per Serving: Calories: 146;Fat: 10.6g;Protein: 4.2g;-Carbs: 11.8g.

Baby Kale And Cabbage Salad

Servings:6 | Cooking Time: 0 Minutes

Ingredients:
- 2 bunches baby kale, thinly sliced
- ½ head green savoy cabbage, cored and thinly sliced
- 1 medium red bell pepper, thinly sliced
- 1 garlic clove, thinly sliced
- 1 cup toasted peanuts
- Dressing:
- Juice of 1 lemon
- ¼ cup apple cider vinegar
- 1 teaspoon ground cumin
- ¼ teaspoon smoked paprika

Directions:
1. In a large mixing bowl, toss together the kale and cabbage.
2. Make the dressing: Whisk together the lemon juice, vinegar, cumin and paprika in a small bowl.
3. Pour the dressing over the greens and gently massage with your hands.
4. Add the pepper, garlic and peanuts to the mixing bowl. Toss to combine.
5. Serve immediately.

Nutrition:
- Info Per Serving: Calories: 199;Fat: 12.0g;Protein: 10.0g;Carbs: 17.0g.

Roasted Asparagus With Hazelnuts

Servings:4 | Cooking Time:25 Minutes

Ingredients:
- 2 tbsp olive oil
- 1 lb asparagus, trimmed
- ¼ cup hazelnuts, chopped
- 1 lemon, juiced and zested
- Salt and black pepper to taste
- ½ tsp red pepper flakes

Directions:
1. Preheat oven to 425ºF. Arrange the asparagus on a baking sheet. Combine olive oil, lemon zest, lemon juice, salt, hazelnuts, and black pepper in a bowl and mix well. Pour the mixture over the asparagus. Place in the oven and roast for 15-20 minutes until tender and lightly charred. Serve topped with red pepper flakes.

Nutrition:
- Info Per Serving: Calories: 112;Fat: 10g;Protein: 3.2g;-Carbs: 5.2g.

Tomatoes Filled With Tabbouleh

Servings:4 | Cooking Time:25 Minutes

Ingredients:
- 3 tbsp olive oil, divided
- 8 medium tomatoes
- ½ cup water
- ½ cup bulgur wheat
- 1 ½ cups minced parsley
- ⅓ cup minced fresh mint
- 2 scallions, chopped
- 1 tsp sumac
- Salt and black pepper to taste
- 1 lemon, zested

Directions:
1. Place the bulgur wheat and 2 cups of salted water in a pot and bring to a boil. Lower the heat and simmer for 10 minutes or until tender. Remove the pot from the heat and cover with a lid. Let it sit for 15 minutes.
2. Preheat the oven to 400ºF. Slice off the top of each tomato and scoop out the pulp and seeds using a spoon into a sieve set over a bowl. Drain and discard any excess liquid; chop the remaining pulp and place it in a large mixing bowl. Add in parsley, mint, scallions, sumac, lemon zest, lemon juice, bulgur, pepper, and salt, and mix well.
3. Spoon the filling into the tomatoes and place the lids on top. Drizzle with olive oil and bake for 15-20 minutes until the tomatoes are tender. Serve and enjoy!

Nutrition:
- Info Per Serving: Calories: 160;Fat: 7g;Protein: 5g;-Carbs: 22g.

Baked Vegetable Stew

Servings:6 | Cooking Time:70 Minutes

Ingredients:
- 1 can diced tomatoes, drained with juice reserved
- 3 tbsp olive oil
- 1 onion, chopped
- 2 tbsp fresh oregano, minced
- 1 tsp paprika
- 4 garlic cloves, minced
- 1 ½ lb green beans, sliced
- 1 lb Yukon Gold potatoes, peeled and chopped
- 1 tbsp tomato paste
- Salt and black pepper to taste
- 3 tbsp fresh basil, chopped

Directions:
1. Preheat oven to 360°F. Warm the olive oil in a skillet over medium heat. Sauté onion and garlic for 3 minutes until softened. Stir in oregano and paprika for 30 seconds. Transfer to a baking dish and add in green beans, potatoes, tomatoes, tomato paste, salt, pepper, and 1 ½ cups of water; stir well. Bake for 40-50 minutes. Sprinkle with basil. Serve.

Nutrition:
- Info Per Serving: Calories: 121;Fat: 0.8g;Protein: 4.2g;-Carbs: 26g.

Spicy Potato Wedges

Servings:4 | Cooking Time:30 Minutes

Ingredients:
- 1 ½ lb potatoes, peeled and cut into wedges
- 3 tbsp olive oil
- 1 tbsp minced fresh rosemary
- 2 tsp chili powder
- 3 garlic cloves, minced
- Salt and black pepper to taste

Directions:
1. Preheat the oven to 370ºF. Toss the wedges with olive oil, garlic, salt, and pepper. Spread out in a roasting sheet. Roast for 15-20 minutes until browned and crisp at the edges. Remove and sprinkle with chili powder and rosemary.

Nutrition:
- Info Per Serving: Calories: 152;Fat: 7g;Protein: 2.5g;-Carbs: 21g.

Minty Broccoli & Walnuts

Servings:2 | Cooking Time:10 Minutes

Ingredients:
- 1 garlic clove, minced
- ½ cups walnuts, chopped
- 3 cups broccoli florets, steamed
- 1 tbsp mint, chopped
- ½ lemon, juiced
- Salt and black pepper to taste

Directions:
1. Mix walnuts, broccoli, garlic, mint, lemon juice, salt, and pepper in a bowl. Serve chilled.

Nutrition:
- Info Per Serving: Calories: 210;Fat: 7g;Protein: 4g;-Carbs: 9g.

Spicy Kale With Almonds

Servings:4 | Cooking Time:25 Minutes

Ingredients:
- 2 tbsp olive oil
- ¼ cup slivered almonds
- 1 lb chopped kale
- ¼ cup vegetable broth
- 1 lemon, juiced and zested
- 1 garlic clove, minced
- 1 tbsp red pepper flakes
- Salt and black pepper to taste

Directions:
1. Warm olive oil in a pan over medium heat and sauté garlic, kale, salt, and pepper for 8-9 minutes until soft. Add in lemon juice, lemon zest, red pepper flakes, and vegetable broth and continue cooking until the liquid evaporates, about 3-5 minutes. Garnish with almonds and serve.

Nutrition:
- Info Per Serving: Calories: 123;Fat: 8.1g;Protein: 4g;-Carbs: 10.8g.

Stir-Fry Baby Bok Choy

Servings:6 | Cooking Time: 10 To 13 Minutes

Ingredients:
- 2 tablespoons coconut oil
- 1 large onion, finely diced
- 2 teaspoons ground cumin
- 1-inch piece fresh ginger, grated
- 1 teaspoon ground turmeric
- ½ teaspoon salt
- 12 baby bok choy heads, ends trimmed and sliced lengthwise
- Water, as needed
- 3 cups cooked brown rice

Directions:
1. Heat the coconut oil in a large pan over medium heat.
2. Sauté the onion for 5 minutes, stirring occasionally, or until the onion is translucent.
3. Fold in the cumin, ginger, turmeric, and salt and stir to coat well.
4. Add the bok choy and cook for 5 to 8 minutes, stirring occasionally, or until the bok choy is tender but crisp. You can add 1 tablespoon of water at a time, if the skillet gets dry until you finish sautéing.
5. Transfer the bok choy to a plate and serve over the cooked brown rice.

Nutrition:
- Info Per Serving: Calories: 443;Fat: 8.8g;Protein: 30.3g;- Carbs: 75.7g.

Homemade Vegetarian Moussaka

Servings:4 | Cooking Time:80 Minutes

Ingredients:
- 2 tbsp olive oil
- 1 yellow onion, chopped
- 2 garlic cloves, chopped
- 2 eggplants, halved
- ½ cup vegetable broth
- Salt and black pepper to taste
- ½ tsp paprika
- ¼ cup parsley, chopped
- 1 tsp basil, chopped
- 1 tsp hot sauce
- 1 tomato, chopped
- 2 tbsp tomato puree
- 6 Kalamata olives, chopped
- ½ cup feta cheese, crumbled

Directions:
1. Preheat oven to 360ºF. Remove the tender center part of the eggplants and chop it. Arrange the eggplant halves on a baking tray and drizzle with some olive oil. Roast for 35-40 minutes.

2. Warm the remaining olive oil in a skillet over medium heat and add eggplant flesh, onion, and garlic and sauté for 5 minutes until tender. Stir in the vegetable broth, salt, pepper, basil, hot sauce, paprika, tomato, and tomato puree. Lower the heat and simmer for 10-15 minutes. Once the eggplants are ready, remove them from the oven and fill them with the mixture. Top with Kalamata olives and feta cheese. Return to the oven and bake for 10-15 minutes. Sprinkle with parsley.

Nutrition:
- Info Per Serving: Calories: 223;Fat: 14g;Protein: 6.9g;- Carbs: 23g.

Sweet Potato Chickpea Buddha Bowl

Servings:2 | Cooking Time: 10 To 15 Minutes

Ingredients:
- Sauce:
- 1 tablespoon tahini
- 2 tablespoons plain Greek yogurt
- 2 tablespoons hemp seeds
- 1 garlic clove, minced
- Pinch salt
- Freshly ground black pepper, to taste
- Bowl:
- 1 small sweet potato, peeled and finely diced
- 1 teaspoon extra-virgin olive oil
- 1 cup from 1 can low-sodium chickpeas, drained and rinsed
- 2 cups baby kale

Directions:
1. Make the Sauce
2. Whisk together the tahini and yogurt in a small bowl.
3. Stir in the hemp seeds and minced garlic. Season with salt pepper. Add 2 to 3 tablespoons water to create a creamy yet pourable consistency and set aside.
4. Make the Bowl
5. Preheat the oven to 425ºF. Line a baking sheet with parchment paper.
6. Place the sweet potato on the prepared baking sheet and drizzle with the olive oil. Toss well
7. Roast in the preheated oven for 10 to 15 minutes, stirring once during cooking, or until fork-tender and browned.
8. In each of 2 bowls, place ½ cup of chickpeas, 1 cup of baby kale, and half of the cooked sweet potato. Serve drizzled with half of the prepared sauce.

Nutrition:
- Info Per Serving: Calories: 323;Fat: 14.1g;Protein: 17.0g;Carbs: 36.0g.

Ratatouille

Servings:4 | Cooking Time: 30 Minutes

Ingredients:
- 4 tablespoons extra-virgin olive oil, divided
- 1 cup diced zucchini
- 2 cups diced eggplant
- 1 cup diced onion
- 1 cup chopped green bell pepper
- 1 can no-salt-added diced tomatoes
- ½ teaspoon garlic powder
- 1 teaspoon ground thyme
- Salt and freshly ground black pepper, to taste

Directions:
1. Heat 2 tablespoons of olive oil in a large saucepan over medium heat until it shimmers.
2. Add the zucchini and eggplant and sauté for 10 minutes, stirring occasionally. If necessary, add the remaining olive oil.
3. Stir in the onion and bell pepper and sauté for 5 minutes until softened.
4. Add the diced tomatoes with their juice, garlic powder, and thyme and stir to combine. Continue cooking for 15 minutes until the vegetables are cooked through, stirring occasionally. Sprinkle with salt and black pepper.
5. Remove from the heat and serve on a plate.

Nutrition:
- Info Per Serving: Calories: 189;Fat: 13.7g;Protein: 3.1g;-Carbs: 14.8g.

Hot Turnip Chickpeas

Servings:4 | Cooking Time:50 Minutes

Ingredients:
- 2 tbsp olive oil
- 2 onions, chopped
- 2 red bell peppers, chopped
- Salt and black pepper to taste
- ¼ cup tomato paste
- 1 jalapeño pepper, minced
- 5 garlic cloves, minced
- ¾ tsp ground cumin
- ¼ tsp cayenne pepper
- 2 cans chickpeas
- 12 oz potatoes, chopped
- ¼ cup chopped fresh parsley
- 1 lemon, juiced

Directions:
1. Warm the olive oil in a saucepan oven over medium heat. Sauté the onions, bell peppers, salt, and pepper for 6 minutes until softened and lightly browned. Stir in tomato paste, jalapeño pepper, garlic, cumin, and cayenne pepper and cook for about 30 seconds until fragrant. Stir in chick-peas and their liquid, potatoes, and 1 cup of water. Bring to simmer and cook for 25-35 minutes until potatoes are tender and the sauce has thickened. Stir in parsley and lemon juice.

Nutrition:
- Info Per Serving: Calories: 124;Fat: 5.3g;Protein: 3.7g;-Carbs: 17g.

Vegan Lentil Bolognese

Servings:2 | Cooking Time: 50 Minutes

Ingredients:
- 1 medium celery stalk
- 1 large carrot
- ½ large onion
- 1 garlic clove
- 2 tablespoons olive oil
- 1 can crushed tomatoes
- 1 cup red wine
- ½ teaspoon salt, plus more as needed
- ½ teaspoon pure maple syrup
- 1 cup cooked lentils (prepared from ½ cup dry)

Directions:
1. Add the celery, carrot, onion, and garlic to a food processor and process until everything is finely chopped.
2. In a Dutch oven, heat the olive oil over medium-high heat. Add the chopped mixture and sauté for about 10 minutes, stirring occasionally, or until the vegetables are lightly browned.
3. Stir in the tomatoes, wine, salt, and maple syrup and bring to a boil.
4. Once the sauce starts to boil, cover, and reduce the heat to medium-low. Simmer for 30 minutes, stirring occasionally, or until the vegetables are softened.
5. Stir in the cooked lentils and cook for an additional 5 minutes until warmed through.
6. Taste and add additional salt, if needed. Serve warm.

Nutrition:
- Info Per Serving: Calories: 367;Fat: 15.0g;Protein: 13.7g;Carbs: 44.5g.

Paprika Cauliflower Steaks With Walnut Sauce

Servings:2 | Cooking Time: 30 Minutes

Ingredients:
- Walnut Sauce:
- ½ cup raw walnut halves
- 2 tablespoons virgin olive oil, divided
- 1 clove garlic, chopped
- 1 small yellow onion, chopped
- ½ cup unsweetened almond milk
- 2 tablespoons fresh lemon juice
- Salt and pepper, to taste
- Paprika Cauliflower:
- 1 medium head cauliflower
- 1 teaspoon sweet paprika
- 1 teaspoon minced fresh thyme leaves

Directions:
1. Preheat the oven to 350ºF.
2. Make the walnut sauce: Toast the walnuts in a large, ovenproof skillet over medium heat until fragrant and slightly darkened, about 5 minutes. Transfer the walnuts to a blender.
3. Heat 1 tablespoon of olive oil in the skillet. Add the garlic and onion and sauté for about 2 minutes, or until slightly softened. Transfer the garlic and onion into the blender, along with the almond milk, lemon juice, salt, and pepper. Blend the ingredients until smooth and creamy. Keep the sauce warm while you prepare the cauliflower.
4. Make the paprika cauliflower: Cut two 1-inch-thick "steaks" from the center of the cauliflower. Lightly moisten the steaks with water and season both sides with paprika, thyme, salt, and pepper.
5. Heat the remaining 1 tablespoon of olive oil in the skillet over medium-high heat. Add the cauliflower steaks and sear for about 3 minutes until evenly browned. Flip the cauliflower steaks and transfer the skillet to the oven.
6. Roast in the preheated oven for about 20 minutes until crisp-tender.
7. Serve the cauliflower steaks warm with the walnut sauce on the side.

Nutrition:
- Info Per Serving: Calories: 367;Fat: 27.9g;Protein: 7.0g;- Carbs: 22.7g.

Stuffed Portobello Mushroom With Tomatoes

Servings:4 | Cooking Time: 15 Minutes

Ingredients:
- 4 large portobello mushroom caps
- 3 tablespoons extra-virgin olive oil
- Salt and freshly ground black pepper, to taste
- 4 sun-dried tomatoes
- 1 cup shredded mozzarella cheese, divided
- ½ to ¾ cup low-sodium tomato sauce

Directions:
1. Preheat the broiler on high.
2. Arrange the mushroom caps on a baking sheet and drizzle with olive oil. Sprinkle with salt and pepper.
3. Broil for 1o minutes, flipping the mushroom caps halfway through, until browned on the top.
4. Remove from the broil. Spoon 1 tomato, 2 tablespoons of cheese, and 2 to 3 tablespoons of sauce onto each mushroom cap.
5. Return the mushroom caps to the broiler and continue broiling for 2 to 3 minutes.
6. Cool for 5 minutes before serving.

Nutrition:
- Info Per Serving: Calories: 217;Fat: 15.8g;Protein: 11.2g;Carbs: 11.7g.

Baked Potato With Veggie Mix

Servings:4 | Cooking Time:45 Minutes

Ingredients:
- 4 tbsp olive oil
- 1 lb potatoes, peeled and diced
- 2 red bell peppers, halved
- 1 lb mushrooms, sliced
- 2 tomatoes, diced
- 8 garlic cloves, peeled
- 1 eggplant, sliced
- 1 yellow onion, quartered
- ½ tsp dried oregano
- ¼ tsp caraway seeds
- Salt to taste

Directions:
1. Preheat the oven to 390°F. In a bowl, combine the bell peppers, mushrooms, tomatoes, eggplant, onion, garlic, salt, olive oil, oregano, and caraway seeds. Set aside. Arrange the potatoes on a baking dish and bake for 15 minutes. Top with the veggies mixture and bake for 15-20 minutes until tender.

Nutrition:
- Info Per Serving: Calories: 302;Fat: 15g;Protein: 8.5g;- Carbs: 39g.

5-ingredient Zucchini Fritters

Servings:14 | Cooking Time: 5 Minutes

Ingredients:
- 4 cups grated zucchini
- Salt, to taste
- 2 large eggs, lightly beaten
- ⅓ cup sliced scallions (green and white parts)
- ⅔ all-purpose flour
- ⅛ teaspoon black pepper
- 2 tablespoons olive oil

Directions:
1. Put the grated zucchini in a colander and lightly season with salt. Set aside to rest for 10 minutes. Squeeze out as much liquid from the grated zucchini as possible.
2. Pour the grated zucchini into a bowl. Fold in the beaten eggs, scallions, flour, salt, and pepper and stir until everything is well combined.
3. Heat the olive oil in a large skillet over medium heat until hot.
4. Drop 3 tablespoons mounds of the zucchini mixture onto the hot skillet to make each fritter, pressing them lightly into rounds and spacing them about 2 inches apart.
5. Cook for 2 to 3 minutes. Flip the zucchini fritters and cook for 2 minutes more, or until they are golden brown and cooked through.
6. Remove from the heat to a plate lined with paper towels. Repeat with the remaining zucchini mixture.
7. Serve hot.

Nutrition:
- Info Per Serving: Calories: 113;Fat: 6.1g;Protein: 4.0g;Carbs: 12.2g.

Baked Tomatoes And Chickpeas

Servings:4 | Cooking Time: 40 To 45 Minutes

Ingredients:
- 1 tablespoon extra-virgin olive oil
- ½ medium onion, chopped
- 3 garlic cloves, chopped
- ¼ teaspoon ground cumin
- 2 teaspoons smoked paprika
- 2 cans chickpeas, drained and rinsed
- 4 cups halved cherry tomatoes
- ½ cup plain Greek yogurt, for serving
- 1 cup crumbled feta cheese, for serving

Directions:
1. Preheat the oven to 425ºF.
2. Heat the olive oil in an ovenproof skillet over medium heat.
3. Add the onion and garlic and sauté for about 5 minutes, stirring occasionally, or until tender and fragrant.
4. Add the paprika and cumin and cook for 2 minutes. Stir in the chickpeas and tomatoes and allow to simmer for 5 to 10 minutes.
5. Transfer the skillet to the preheated oven and roast for 25 to 30 minutes, or until the mixture bubbles and thickens.
6. Remove from the oven and serve topped with yogurt and crumbled feta cheese.

Nutrition:
- Info Per Serving: Calories: 411;Fat: 14.9g;Protein: 20.2g;Carbs: 50.7g.

Roasted Vegetable Medley

Servings:2 | Cooking Time:65 Minutes

Ingredients:
- 1 head garlic, cloves split apart, unpeeled
- 3 tbsp olive oil
- 2 carrots, cut into strips
- ¼ lb asparagus, chopped
- ½ lb Brussels sprouts, halved
- 2 cups broccoli florets
- 1 cup cherry tomatoes
- ½ fresh lemon, sliced
- Salt and black pepper to taste

Directions:
1. Preheat oven to 375ºF. Drizzle the garlic cloves with some olive oil and lightly wrap them in a small piece of foil. Place the packet in the oven and roast for 30 minutes. Place all the vegetables and the lemon slices into a large mixing bowl. Drizzle with the remaining olive oil and season with salt and pepper. Increase the oven to 400 F. Pour the vegetables on a sheet pan in a single layer, leaving the packet of garlic cloves on the pan. Roast for 20 minutes, shaking occasionally until tender. Remove the pan from the oven. Let the garlic cloves sit until cool enough to handle, then remove the skins. Top the vegetables with roasted garlic and serve.

Nutrition:
- Info Per Serving: Calories: 256;Fat: 15g;Protein: 7g;Carbs: 31g.

Sautéed Spinach And Leeks

Servings:2 | Cooking Time: 8 Minutes

Ingredients:
- 3 tablespoons olive oil
- 2 garlic cloves, crushed
- 2 leeks, chopped
- 2 red onions, chopped
- 9 ounces fresh spinach
- 1 teaspoon kosher salt
- ½ cup crumbled goat cheese

Directions:
1. Coat the bottom of the Instant Pot with the olive oil.
2. Add the garlic, leek, and onions and stir-fry for about 5 minutes, on Sauté mode.
3. Stir in the spinach. Sprinkle with the salt and sauté for an additional 3 minutes, stirring constantly.
4. Transfer to a plate and scatter with the goat cheese before serving.

Nutrition:
- Info Per Serving: Calories: 447;Fat: 31.2g;Protein: 14.6g;Carbs: 28.7g.

Asparagus & Mushroom Farro

Servings:2 | Cooking Time:40 Minutes

Ingredients:
- ½ oz dried porcini mushrooms, soaked
- 2 tbsp olive oil
- 1 cup hot water
- 3 cups vegetable stock
- ½ large onion, minced
- 1 garlic clove
- 1 cup fresh mushrooms, sliced
- ½ cup farro
- ½ cup dry white wine
- ½ tsp dried thyme
- ½ tsp dried marjoram
- 4 oz asparagus, chopped
- 2 tbsp grated Parmesan cheese

Directions:
1. Drain the soaked mushrooms, reserving the liquid, and cut them into slices. Warm the olive oil in a saucepan oven over medium heat. Sauté the onion, garlic, and soaked and fresh mushrooms for 8 minutes. Stir in the farro for 1-2 minutes. Add the wine, thyme, marjoram, reserved mushroom liquid, and a ladleful of stock. Bring it to a boil.
2. Lower the heat and cook for about 20 minutes, stirring occasionally and adding another ladleful of stock, until the farro is cooked through but not overcooked. Stir in the asparagus and the remaining stock. Cook for 3-5 more minutes or until the asparagus is softened. Sprinkle with Parmesan cheese and serve warm.

Nutrition:
- Info Per Serving: Calories: 341;Fat: 16g;Protein: 13g;-Carbs: 26g.

Fried Eggplant Rolls

Servings:4 | Cooking Time: 10 Minutes

Ingredients:
- 2 large eggplants, trimmed and cut lengthwise into ¼-inch-thick slices
- 1 teaspoon salt
- 1 cup shredded ricotta cheese
- 4 ounces goat cheese, shredded
- ¼ cup finely chopped fresh basil
- ½ teaspoon freshly ground black pepper
- Olive oil spray

Directions:
1. Add the eggplant slices to a colander and season with salt. Set aside for 15 to 20 minutes.
2. Mix together the ricotta and goat cheese, basil, and black pepper in a large bowl and stir to combine. Set aside.
3. Dry the eggplant slices with paper towels and lightly mist them with olive oil spray.
4. Heat a large skillet over medium heat and lightly spray it with olive oil spray.
5. Arrange the eggplant slices in the skillet and fry each side for 3 minutes until golden brown.
6. Remove from the heat to a paper towel-lined plate and rest for 5 minutes.
7. Make the eggplant rolls: Lay the eggplant slices on a flat work surface and top each slice with a tablespoon of the prepared cheese mixture. Roll them up and serve immediately.

Nutrition:
- Info Per Serving: Calories: 254;Fat: 14.9g;Protein: 15.3g;Carbs: 18.6g.

Roasted Artichokes

Servings:4 | Cooking Time:50 Minutes

Ingredients:

- 4 artichokes, stalk trimmed and large leaves removed
- 2 lemons, freshly squeezed
- 4 tbsp extra-virgin olive oil
- 4 cloves garlic, chopped
- 1 tsp fresh rosemary
- 1 tsp fresh basil
- 1 tsp fresh parsley
- 1 tsp fresh oregano
- Salt and black pepper to taste
- 1 tsp red pepper flakes
- 1 tsp paprika

Directions:

1. Preheat oven to 395ºF. In a small bowl, thoroughly combine the garlic with herbs and spices; set aside. Cut the artichokes in half vertically and scoop out the fibrous choke to expose the heart with a teaspoon.
2. Rub the lemon juice all over the entire surface of the artichoke halves. Arrange them on a parchment-lined baking dish, cut side up, and brush them evenly with olive oil. Stuff the cavities with the garlic/herb mixture. Cover them with aluminum foil and bake for 30 minutes. Discard the foil and bake for another 10 minutes until lightly charred. Serve.

Nutrition:

- Info Per Serving: Calories: 220;Fat: 14g;Protein: 6g;-Carbs: 21g.

Parmesan Asparagus With Tomatoes

Servings:6 | Cooking Time:30 Minutes

Ingredients:

- 3 tbsp olive oil
- 2 garlic cloves, minced
- 12 oz cherry tomatoes, halved
- 1 tsp dried oregano
- 10 Kalamata olives, chopped
- 2 lb asparagus, trimmed
- 2 tbsp fresh basil, chopped
- ¼ cup Parmesan cheese, grated
- Salt and black pepper to taste

Directions:

1. Warm 2 tbsp of olive oil in a skillet over medium heat sauté the garlic for 1-2 minutes, stirring often, until golden. Add tomatoes, olives, and oregano and cook until tomatoes begin to break down, about 3 minutes; transfer to a bowl.
2. Coat the asparagus with the remaining olive oil and cook in a grill pan over medium heat for about 5 minutes, turning once until crisp-tender. Sprinkle with salt and pepper. Transfer asparagus to a serving platter, top with tomato

mixture, and sprinkle with basil and Parmesan cheese. Serve and enjoy!

Nutrition:

- Info Per Serving: Calories: 157;Fat: 7g;Protein: 7.3g;-Carbs: 19g.

Steamed Beetroot With Nutty Yogurt

Servings:4 | Cooking Time:30 Min + Chilling Time

Ingredients:

- ¼ cup extra virgin olive oil
- 1 lb beetroots, cut into wedges
- 1 cup Greek yogurt
- 3 spring onions, sliced
- 5 dill pickles, finely chopped
- 2 garlic cloves, minced
- 2 tbsp fresh parsley, chopped
- 1 oz mixed nuts, crushed
- Salt to taste

Directions:

1. In a pot over medium heat, insert a steamer basket and pour in 1 cup of water. Place in the beetroots and steam for 10-15 minutes until tender. Remove to a plate and let cool. In a bowl, combine the pickles, spring onions, garlic, salt, 3 tbsp of olive oil, Greek yogurt, and nuts and mix well. Spread the yogurt mixture on a serving plate and arrange the beetroot wedges on top. Drizzle with the remaining olive oil and top with parsley. Serve and enjoy!

Nutrition:

- Info Per Serving: Calories: 271;Fat: 18g;Protein: 9.6g;-Carbs: 22g.

Grilled Vegetable Skewers

Servings:4 | Cooking Time: 10 Minutes

Ingredients:

- 4 medium red onions, peeled and sliced into 6 wedges
- 4 medium zucchini, cut into 1-inch-thick slices
- 2 beefsteak tomatoes, cut into quarters
- 4 red bell peppers, cut into 2-inch squares
- 2 orange bell peppers, cut into 2-inch squares
- 2 yellow bell peppers, cut into 2-inch squares
- 2 tablespoons plus 1 teaspoon olive oil, divided
- SPECIAL EQUIPMENT:
- 4 wooden skewers, soaked in water for at least 30 minutes

Directions:

1. Preheat the grill to medium-high heat.
2. Skewer the vegetables by alternating between red onion, zucchini, tomatoes, and the different colored bell peppers. Brush them with 2 tablespoons of olive oil.
3. Oil the grill grates with 1 teaspoon of olive oil and grill

the vegetable skewers for 5 minutes. Flip the skewers and grill for 5 minutes more, or until they are cooked to your liking.

4. Let the skewers cool for 5 minutes before serving.

Nutrition:
• Info Per Serving: Calories: 115;Fat: 3.0g;Protein: 3.5g;-Carbs: 18.7g.

Sweet Mustard Cabbage Hash

Servings:4 | Cooking Time:30 Minutes

Ingredients:
• 1 head Savoy cabbage, shredded
• 3 tbsp olive oil
• 1 onion, finely chopped
• 2 garlic cloves, minced
• ½ tsp fennel seeds
• ¼ cup red wine vinegar
• 1 tbsp mustard powder
• 1 tbsp honey
• Salt and black pepper to taste

Directions:
1. Warm olive oil in a pan over medium heat and sauté onion, fennel seeds, cabbage, salt, and pepper for 8-9 minutes.
2. In a bowl, mix vinegar, mustard, and honey; set aside. Sauté garlic in the pan for 30 seconds. Pour in vinegar mixture and cook for 10-15 minutes until the liquid reduces by half.

Nutrition:
• Info Per Serving: Calories: 181;Fat: 12g;Protein: 3.4g;-Carbs: 19g.

Brussels Sprouts Linguine

Servings:4 | Cooking Time: 25 Minutes

Ingredients:
• 8 ounces whole-wheat linguine
• ⅓ cup plus 2 tablespoons extra-virgin olive oil, divided
• 1 medium sweet onion, diced
• 2 to 3 garlic cloves, smashed
• 8 ounces Brussels sprouts, chopped
• ½ cup chicken stock
• ⅓ cup dry white wine
• ½ cup shredded Parmesan cheese
• 1 lemon, quartered

Directions:
1. Bring a large pot of water to a boil and cook the pasta for about 5 minutes, or until al dente. Drain the pasta and reserve 1 cup of the pasta water. Mix the cooked pasta with 2 tablespoons of the olive oil. Set aside.
2. In a large skillet, heat the remaining ⅓ cup of the olive

oil over medium heat. Add the onion to the skillet and sauté for about 4 minutes, or until tender. Add the smashed garlic cloves and sauté for 1 minute, or until fragrant.
3. Stir in the Brussels sprouts and cook covered for 10 minutes. Pour in the chicken stock to prevent burning. Once the Brussels sprouts have wilted and are fork-tender, add white wine and cook for about 5 minutes, or until reduced.
4. Add the pasta to the skillet and add the pasta water as needed.
5. Top with the Parmesan cheese and squeeze the lemon over the dish right before eating.

Nutrition:
• Info Per Serving: Calories: 502;Fat: 31.0g;Protein: 15.0g;Carbs: 50.0g.

Simple Honey-glazed Baby Carrots

Servings:2 | Cooking Time: 6 Minutes

Ingredients:
• ⅔ cup water
• 1½ pounds baby carrots
• 4 tablespoons almond butter
• ½ cup honey
• 1 teaspoon dried thyme
• 1½ teaspoons dried dill
• Salt, to taste

Directions:
1. Pour the water into the Instant Pot and add a steamer basket. Place the baby carrots in the basket.
2. Secure the lid. Select the Manual mode and set the cooking time for 4 minutes at High Pressure.
3. Once cooking is complete, do a quick pressure release. Carefully open the lid.
4. Transfer the carrots to a plate and set aside.
5. Pour the water out of the Instant Pot and dry it.
6. Press the Sauté button on the Instant Pot and heat the almond butter.
7. Stir in the honey, thyme, and dill.
8. Return the carrots to the Instant Pot and stir until well coated. Sauté for another 1 minute.
9. Taste and season with salt as needed. Serve warm.

Nutrition:
• Info Per Serving: Calories: 575;Fat: 23.5g;Protein: 2.8g;-Carbs: 90.6g.

Cauliflower Cakes With Goat Cheese

Servings:4 | Cooking Time:50 Minutes

Ingredients:
- ¼ cup olive oil
- 10 oz cauliflower florets
- 1 tsp ground turmeric
- 1 tsp ground coriander
- Salt and black pepper to taste
- ½ tsp ground mustard seeds
- 4 oz Goat cheese, softened
- 2 scallions, sliced thin
- 1 large egg, lightly beaten
- 2 garlic cloves, minced
- 1 tsp grated lemon zest
- 4 lemon wedges
- ¼ cup flour

Directions:
1. Preheat oven to 420°F. In a bowl, whisk 1 tablespoon oil, turmeric, coriander, salt, ground mustard, and pepper. Add in the cauliflower and toss to coat. Transfer to a greased baking sheet and spread it in a single layer. Roast for 20-25 minutes until cauliflower is well browned and tender. Transfer the cauliflower to a large bowl and mash it coarsely with a potato masher. Stir in Goat cheese, scallions, egg, garlic, and lemon zest until well combined. Sprinkle flour over cauliflower mixture and stir to incorporate. Shape the mixture into 10-12 cakes and place them on a sheet pan. Chill to firm, about 30 minutes. Warm the remaining olive oil in a skillet over medium heat. Fry the cakes for 5-6 minutes on each side until deep golden brown and crisp. Serve with lemon wedges.

Nutrition:
- Info Per Serving: Calories: 320;Fat: 25g;Protein: 13g;-Carbs: 12g.

Simple Braised Carrots

Servings:4 | Cooking Time:20 Minutes

Ingredients:
- 2 tbsp butter
- 1 lb carrots, cut into sticks
- ¾ cup water
- ¼ cup orange juice
- 1 tbsp honey
- Salt and white pepper to taste
- 1 tsp rosemary leaves

Directions:
1. Combine all the ingredients, except for the carrots and rosemary, in a heavy saucepan over medium heat and bring to a boil. Add carrots and cover. Turn the heat to a simmer and continue to cook for 5–8 minutes until carrots are soft when pierced with a knife. Remove the carrots to a serving plate. Then, increase heat to high and bring the liquid to a boil. Boil until the liquid has reduced and syrupy, about 4 minutes. Drizzle the sauce over the carrots and sprinkle with rosemary. Serve warm.

Nutrition:
- Info Per Serving: Calories: 122;Fat: 6g;Protein: 1g;-Carbs: 17g.

Chili Vegetable Skillet

Servings:4 | Cooking Time:30 Minutes

Ingredients:
- 1 cup condensed cream of mushroom soup
- 1 ½ lb eggplants, cut into chunks
- 1 cup cremini mushrooms, sliced
- 4 tbsp olive oil
- 1 carrot, thinly sliced
- 1 can tomatoes
- ½ cup red onion, thinly sliced
- 2 garlic cloves, minced
- 1 tsp fresh rosemary
- 1 tsp chili pepper
- Salt and black pepper to taste
- 2 tbsp parsley, chopped
- ¼ cup Parmesan cheese, grated

Directions:
1. Warm the olive oil in a skillet over medium heat. Add in the eggplant and cook until golden brown on all sides, about 5 minutes; set aside. Add in the carrot, onion, and mushrooms and sauté for 4 more minutes to the same skillet. Add in garlic, rosemary, and chili pepper. Cook for another 30-40 seconds. Add in 1 cup of water, cream of mushroom soup, and tomatoes. Bring to a boil and lower the heat; simmer covered for 5 minutes. Mix in sautéed eggplants and parsley and cook for 10 more minutes. Sprinkle with salt and black pepper. Serve topped with Parmesan cheese.

Nutrition:
- Info Per Serving: Calories: 261;Fat: 18.7g;Protein: 5g;-Carbs: 23g.

Vegetable And Tofu Scramble

Servings:2 | Cooking Time: 10 Minutes

Ingredients:
- 2 tablespoons extra-virgin olive oil
- ½ red onion, finely chopped
- 1 cup chopped kale
- 8 ounces mushrooms, sliced
- 8 ounces tofu, cut into pieces
- 2 garlic cloves, minced
- Pinch red pepper flakes
- ½ teaspoon sea salt
- ⅛ teaspoon freshly ground black pepper

Directions:
1. Heat the olive oil in a medium nonstick skillet over medium-high heat until shimmering.
2. Add the onion, kale, and mushrooms to the skillet and cook for about 5 minutes, stirring occasionally, or until the vegetables start to brown.
3. Add the tofu and stir-fry for 3 to 4 minutes until softened.
4. Stir in the garlic, red pepper flakes, salt, and black pepper and cook for 30 seconds.
5. Let the mixture cool for 5 minutes before serving.

Nutrition:
- Info Per Serving: Calories: 233;Fat: 15.9g;Protein: 13.4g;Carbs: 11.9g.

Cauliflower Hash With Carrots

Servings:4 | Cooking Time: 10 Minutes

Ingredients:
- 3 tablespoons extra-virgin olive oil
- 1 large onion, chopped
- 1 tablespoon minced garlic
- 2 cups diced carrots
- 4 cups cauliflower florets
- ½ teaspoon ground cumin
- 1 teaspoon salt

Directions:
1. In a large skillet, heat the olive oil over medium heat.
2. Add the onion and garlic and sauté for 1 minute. Stir in the carrots and stir-fry for 3 minutes.
3. Add the cauliflower florets, cumin, and salt and toss to combine.
4. Cover and cook for 3 minutes until lightly browned. Stir well and cook, uncovered, for 3 to 4 minutes, until softened.
5. Remove from the heat and serve warm.

Nutrition:
- Info Per Serving: Calories: 158;Fat: 10.8g;Protein: 3.1g;Carbs: 14.9g.

Garlicky Broccoli Rabe

Servings:4 | Cooking Time: 5 To 6 Minutes

Ingredients:
- 14 ounces broccoli rabe, trimmed and cut into 1-inch pieces
- 2 teaspoons salt, plus more for seasoning
- Black pepper, to taste
- 2 tablespoons extra-virgin olive oil
- 3 garlic cloves, minced
- ¼ teaspoon red pepper flakes

Directions:
1. Bring 3 quarts water to a boil in a large saucepan. Add the broccoli rabe and 2 teaspoons of the salt to the boiling water and cook for 2 to 3 minutes, or until wilted and tender.
2. Drain the broccoli rabe. Transfer to ice water and let sit until chilled. Drain again and pat dry.
3. In a skillet over medium heat, heat the oil and add the garlic and red pepper flakes. Sauté for about 2 minutes, or until the garlic begins to sizzle.
4. Increase the heat to medium-high. Stir in the broccoli rabe and cook for about 1 minute, or until heated through, stirring constantly. Season with salt and pepper.
5. Serve immediately.

Nutrition:
- Info Per Serving: Calories: 87;Fat: 7.3g;Protein: 3.4g;Carbs: 4.0g.

Sides , Salads, And Soups

Sides , Salads, And Soups

Rice Stuffed Bell Peppers

Servings:4 | Cooking Time:70 Minutes

Ingredients:
- 4 red bell peppers, tops and seeds removed
- 2 tbsp olive oil
- 1 cup cooked brown rice
- 4 oz crumbled feta cheese
- 4 cups fresh baby spinach
- 3 Roma tomatoes, chopped
- 1 onion, finely chopped
- 1 cup mushrooms, sliced
- 2 garlic cloves, minced
- 1 tsp dried oregano
- Salt and black pepper to taste
- 2 tbsp fresh parsley, chopped

Directions:
1. Preheat oven to 350° F. Warm olive oil in a skillet over medium heat and sauté onion, garlic, and mushrooms for 5 minutes. Stir in tomatoes, spinach, rice, salt, oregano, parsley, and pepper, cook for 3 minutes until the spinach wilts. Remove from the heat. Stuff the bell peppers with the rice mixture and top with feta cheese. Arrange the peppers on a greased baking pan and pour in 1/4 cup of water. Bake covered with aluminum foil for 30 minutes. Then, bake uncovered for another 10 minutes. Serve and enjoy!

Nutrition:
- Info Per Serving: Calories: 387;Fat: 15g;Protein: 12g;-Carbs: 55g.

Green Garden Salad

Servings:4 | Cooking Time:10 Minutes

Ingredients:
- ¼ cup extra-virgin olive oil
- 2 green onions, sliced
- ½ tsp fresh lemon zest
- 3 tbsp balsamic vinegar
- Salt to taste
- 2 cups baby spinach
- 1 cup watercress
- 1 cup arugula
- 1 celery stick, sliced

Directions:
1. In a small bowl, whisk together the lemon zest, balsamic vinegar, olive oil, and salt. Put the remaining ingredients in a large bowl. Pour the dressing over the salad and lightly toss to coat. Serve and enjoy!

Nutrition:
- Info Per Serving: Calories: 172;Fat: 14g;Protein: 4.1g;-Carbs: 9.8g.

Italian Spinach & Rice Soup

Servings:6 | Cooking Time:65 Minutes

Ingredients:
- 3 tbsp olive oil
- 1 large onion, chopped
- 2 cloves garlic, minced
- 2 lb spinach leaves, chopped
- 6 cups chicken broth
- ½ cup arborio rice
- Salt and black pepper to taste
- 2 oz shaved Parmesan cheese

Directions:
1. Warm the olive oil in a large pot oven over medium heat and add the onion and garlic. Cook until the onions are soft and translucent, about 5 minutes. Add the spinach and stir. Cover the pot and cook the spinach until wilted, about 3 more minutes. With a slotted spoon, remove the spinach and onions from the pot, leaving the liquid.
2. Transfer the spinach mixture to your food processor and process until smooth, then return to the pot. Add the chicken broth and bring to a boil. Add the rice, reduce heat, and simmer until the rice is tender, about 20 minutes. Adjust the taste. Serve topped with Parmesan shavings.

Nutrition:
- Info Per Serving: Calories: 157;Fat: 3.6g;Protein: 8g;-Carbs: 27.1g.

Cheese & Broccoli Quiche

Servings:4 | Cooking Time:45 Minutes

Ingredients:
- 1 tsp Mediterranean seasoning
- 3 eggs
- ½ cup heavy cream
- 3 tbsp olive oil
- 1 red onion, chopped
- 2 garlic cloves, minced
- 2 oz mozzarella, shredded
- 1 lb broccoli, cut into florets

Directions:
1. Preheat oven to 320° F. Warm the oil in a pan over medium heat. Sauté the onion and garlic until just tender

and fragrant. Add in the broccoli and continue to cook until crisp-tender for about 4 minutes. Spoon the mixture into a greased casserole dish. Beat the eggs with heavy cream and Mediterranean seasoning. Spoon this mixture over the broccoli layer. Bake for 18-20 minutes. Top with the shredded cheese and broil for 5 to 6 minutes or until hot and bubbly on the top. Serve.

Nutrition:
• Info Per Serving: Calories: 198;Fat: 14g;Protein: 5g;-Carbs: 12g.

Paella Soup

Servings:6 | Cooking Time: 24 Minutes

Ingredients:
• 2 tablespoons extra-virgin olive oil
• 1 cup chopped onion
• 1½ cups coarsely chopped green bell pepper
• 1½ cups coarsely chopped red bell pepper
• 2 garlic cloves, chopped
• 1 teaspoon ground turmeric
• 1 teaspoon dried thyme
• 2 teaspoons smoked paprika
• 2½ cups uncooked instant brown rice
• 2 cups low-sodium or no-salt-added chicken broth
• 2½ cups water
• 1 cup frozen green peas, thawed
• 1 can low-sodium or no-salt-added crushed tomatoes
• 1 pound fresh raw medium shrimp, shells and tails removed

Directions:
1. In a large stockpot over medium-high heat, heat the oil. Add the onion, bell peppers, and garlic. Cook for 8 minutes, stirring occasionally. Add the turmeric, thyme, and smoked paprika, and cook for 2 minutes more, stirring often. Stir in the rice, broth, and water. Bring to a boil over high heat. Cover, reduce the heat to medium-low, and cook for 10 minutes.
2. Stir the peas, tomatoes, and shrimp into the soup. Cook for 4 minutes, until the shrimp is cooked, turning from gray to pink and white. The soup will be very thick, almost like stew, when ready to serve.
3. Ladle the soup into bowls and serve hot.

Nutrition:
• Info Per Serving: Calories: 431;Fat: 5.7g;Protein: 26.0g;-Carbs: 69.1g.

Herby Yogurt Sauce

Servings:4 | Cooking Time:5 Minutes

Ingredients:
• ¼ tsp fresh lemon juice
• 1 cup plain yogurt
• 2 tbsp fresh cilantro, minced
• 2 tbsp fresh mint, minced
• 1 garlic clove, minced
• Salt and black pepper to taste

Directions:
1. Place the lemon juice, yogurt, cilantro, mint, and garlic together in a bowl and mix well. Season with salt and pepper. Let sit for about 30 minutes to blend the flavors. Store in an airtight container in the refrigerator for up to 2-3 days.

Nutrition:
• Info Per Serving: Calories: 46;Fat: 0.8g;Protein: 3.6g;-Carbs: 4.8g.

Zesty Spanish Potato Salad

Servings:6 | Cooking Time: 5 To 7 Minutes

Ingredients:
• 4 russet potatoes, peeled and chopped
• 3 large hard-boiled eggs, chopped
• 1 cup frozen mixed vegetables, thawed
• ½ cup plain, unsweetened, full-fat Greek yogurt
• 5 tablespoons pitted Spanish olives
• ½ teaspoon freshly ground black pepper
• ½ teaspoon dried mustard seed
• ½ tablespoon freshly squeezed lemon juice
• ½ teaspoon dried dill
• Salt, to taste

Directions:
1. Place the potatoes in a large pot of water and boil for 5 to 7 minutes, until just fork-tender, checking periodically for doneness. You don't have to overcook them.
2. Meanwhile, in a large bowl, mix the eggs, vegetables, yogurt, olives, pepper, mustard, lemon juice, and dill. Season with salt to taste. Once the potatoes are cooled somewhat, add them to the large bowl, then toss well and serve.

Nutrition:
• Info Per Serving: Calories: 192;Fat: 5.0g;Protein: 9.0g;-Carbs: 30.0g.

Greens, Fennel, And Pear Soup With Cashews

Servings:4 | Cooking Time: 15 Minutes

Ingredients:
- 2 tablespoons olive oil
- 1 fennel bulb, cut into ¼-inch-thick slices
- 2 leeks, white part only, sliced
- 2 pears, peeled, cored, and cut into ½-inch cubes
- 1 teaspoon sea salt
- ¼ teaspoon freshly ground black pepper
- ½ cup cashews
- 2 cups packed blanched spinach
- 3 cups low-sodium vegetable soup

Directions:
1. Heat the olive oil in a stockpot over high heat until shimmering.
2. Add the fennel and leeks, then sauté for 5 minutes or until tender.
3. Add the pears and sprinkle with salt and pepper, then sauté for another 3 minutes or until the pears are soft.
4. Add the cashews, spinach, and vegetable soup. Bring to a boil. Reduce the heat to low. Cover and simmer for 5 minutes.
5. Pour the soup in a food processor, then pulse until creamy and smooth.
6. Pour the soup back to the pot and heat over low heat until heated through.
7. Transfer the soup to a large serving bowl and serve immediately.

Nutrition:
- Info Per Serving: Calories: 266;Fat: 15.1g;Protein: 5.2g;-Carbs: 32.9g.

Collard Green & Rice Salad

Servings:4 | Cooking Time:10 Minutes

Ingredients:
- 1 tbsp olive oil
- 1 cup white rice
- 10 oz collard greens, torn
- 4 tbsp walnuts, chopped
- 2 tbsp balsamic vinegar
- 4 tbsp tahini paste
- Salt and black pepper to taste
- 2 tbsp parsley, chopped

Directions:
1. Bring to a boil salted water over medium heat. Add in the rice and cook for 15-18 minutes. Drain and rest to cool.
2. Whisk tahini, 4 tbsp of cold water, and vinegar in a bowl. In a separate bowl, combine cooled rice, collard greens, walnuts, salt, pepper, olive oil, and tahini dressing. Serve topped with parsley.

Nutrition:
- Info Per Serving: Calories: 180;Fat: 4g;Protein: 4g;-Carbs: 6g.

The Ultimate Chicken Bean Soup

Servings:6 | Cooking Time:40 Minutes

Ingredients:
- 3 tbsp olive oil
- 3 garlic cloves, minced
- 1 onion, chopped
- 3 tomatoes, chopped
- 4 cups chicken stock
- 1 lb chicken breasts, cubed
- 1 red chili pepper, chopped
- 1 tbsp fennel seeds, crushed
- 14 oz canned white beans
- 1 lime, zested and juiced
- Salt and black pepper to taste
- 2 tbsp parsley, chopped

Directions:
1. Warm the olive oil in a pot over medium heat. Cook the onion and garlic, adding a splash of water, for 10 minutes until aromatic. Add in the chicken and chili pepper and sit-fry for another 6-8 minutes. Put in tomatoes, chicken stock, beans, lime zest, lime juice, salt, pepper, and fennel seeds and bring to a boil; cook for 30 minutes. Serve topped with parsley.

Nutrition:
- Info Per Serving: Calories: 670;Fat: 18g;Protein: 56g;-Carbs: 74g.

Greek Salad

Servings:4 | Cooking Time:10 Minutes

Ingredients:
- 2 tbsp extra-virgin olive oil
- 2 tomatoes, chopped
- ½ cup grated feta cheese
- 1 green bell pepper, chopped
- 10 Kalamata olives, chopped
- 1 red onion, thinly sliced
- 1 cucumber, chopped
- 2 tbsp apple cider vinegar
- 1 tbsp dried oregano
- Salt and black pepper to taste
- 2 tbsp fresh parsley, chopped

Directions:
1. In a salad bowl, combine bell pepper, red onion, tomatoes, cucumber, and olives. Mix the olive oil, apple cider vinegar, oregano, salt, and pepper in another bowl. Pour the dressing over the salad and toss to combine. Top with

the feta cheese and sprinkle with parsley to serve.

Nutrition:
• Info Per Serving: Calories: 172;Fat: 13g;Protein: 4.4g;-Carbs: 12g.

Egg & Potato Salad

Servings:6 | Cooking Time:25 Minutes

Ingredients:
• ¼ cup olive oil
• 2 lb potatoes, peeled and sliced
• 4 spring onions, chopped
• ½ cup fennel, sliced
• 2 eggs
• 2 tbsp fresh lemon juice
• 1 tbsp capers
• ½ tbsp Dijon mustard
• Salt and black pepper to taste

Directions:
1. Add the eggs to a pot and cover with salted water. Bring to a boil and turn the heat off. Let sit covered in hot water for 10 minutes, then cool before peeling and cutting into slices. In another pot, place the potatoes and cover them with enough water. Bring to a boil, then lower the heat and simmer for 8-10 minutes until tender.
2. In a serving bowl, whisk the olive oil with lemon juice, mustard, salt, and pepper. Add in the potatoes, eggs, capers, spring onions, and fennel slices and toss to combine. Serve.

Nutrition:
• Info Per Serving: Calories: 183;Fat: 10.6g;Protein: 4g;-Carbs: 20g.

Divine Fennel & Zucchini Salad

Servings:4 | Cooking Time:10 Minutes

Ingredients:
• 2 tbsp olive oil
• 1 cup fennel bulb, sliced
• 1 red onion, sliced
• 2 zucchinis, cut into ribbons
• Salt and black pepper to taste
• 2 tsp white wine vinegar
• 1 tsp lemon juice

Directions:
1. In a large bowl, combine fennel, zucchini, red onion, salt, pepper, olive oil, vinegar, and lemon juice and toss to coat.

Nutrition:
• Info Per Serving: Calories: 200;Fat: 4g;Protein: 3g;-Carbs: 4g.

Vegetarian Mediterranean Stew

Servings:4 | Cooking Time:25 Minutes

Ingredients:
• 1 can garbanzo beans, drained and rinsed
• 1 can cannellini beans, drained and rinsed
• 1 ½ cups artichoke hearts, quartered
• 2 cups roasted tomatoes
• 3 tbsp olive oil
• 3 garlic cloves minced
• 1 cup spinach, chopped
• 1 cup vegetable broth
• 4 tbsp Parmesan, grated
• 1 tsp red pepper flakes
• 1 tsp dried oregano
• Salt and black pepper to taste
• 4 sun-dried tomatoes, chopped
• 1 tbsp parsley, chopped
• 1 cup garlic-seasoned croutons
• 2 tbsp feta cheese, crumbled
• 1 tbsp oregano, chopped

Directions:
1. Warm the olive oil in a pot over medium heat and sauté the garlic for 2–3 minutes until golden. Lower the heat to low. Add in the garbanzo beans, cannellini beans, roasted tomatoes, artichoke hearts, spinach, broth, Parmesan cheese, red pepper flakes, oregano, salt, and pepper. Cook and stir for about 10 minutes. Serve warm in individual bowls garnished with sun-dried tomatoes, parsley, croutons, feta cheese, and oregano.

Nutrition:
• Info Per Serving: Calories: 452;Fat: 16g;Protein: 21g;-Carbs: 65g.

Italian-style Chicken Stew

Servings:4 | Cooking Time:20 Minutes

Ingredients:
• 2 fire-roasted tomatoes, peeled, chopped
• 2 lb chicken wings
• 2 potatoes, peeled and chopped
• 1 carrot, chopped
• 2 garlic cloves, chopped
• 2 tbsp olive oil
• 1 tsp smoked paprika, ground
• 4 cups chicken broth
• 2 tbsp fresh parsley, chopped
• Salt and black pepper to taste
• 1 cup spinach, chopped

Directions:
1. Preheat your Instant Pot on Sauté mode. Rub the chicken with salt, pepper, and paprika, and place in the pot. Stir in all remaining ingredients. Seal the lid and cook on High

Pressure for 8 minutes. When ready, do a quick release.

Nutrition:
• Info Per Serving: Calories: 626;Fat: 26g;Protein: 74g;-Carbs: 23g.

Citrus Salad With Kale And Fennel

Servings:2 | Cooking Time: 0 Minutes

Ingredients:
• Dressing:
• 3 tablespoons olive oil
• 2 tablespoons fresh orange juice
• 1 tablespoon blood orange vinegar, other orange vinegar, or cider vinegar
• 1 tablespoon honey
• Salt and freshly ground black pepper, to taste
• Salad:
• 2 cups packed baby kale
• 1 medium navel or blood orange, segmented
• ½ small fennel bulb, stems and leaves removed, sliced into matchsticks
• 3 tablespoons toasted pecans, chopped
• 2 ounces goat cheese, crumbled

Directions:
1. Make the Dressing
2. Mix the olive oil, orange juice, vinegar, and honey in a small bowl and whisk to combine. Season with salt and pepper to taste. Set aside.
3. Make the Salad
4. Divide the baby kale, orange segments, fennel, pecans, and goat cheese evenly between two plates.
5. Drizzle half of the dressing over each salad, and serve.

Nutrition:
• Info Per Serving: Calories: 503;Fat: 39.1g;Protein: 13.2g;Carbs: 31.2g.

Paprika Bean Soup

Servings:4 | Cooking Time:50 Minutes

Ingredients:
• 2 tbsp olive oil
• 6 cups veggie stock
• 1 cup celery, chopped
• 1 cup carrots, chopped
• 1 yellow onion, chopped
• 2 garlic cloves, minced
• ½ cup navy beans, soaked
• 2 tbsp chopped parsley
• ½ tsp paprika
• 1 tsp thyme
• Salt and black pepper to taste

Directions:

1. Warm olive oil in a saucepan and sauté onion, garlic, carrots, and celery for 5 minutes, stirring occasionally. Stir in paprika, thyme, salt, and pepper for 1 minute. Pour in broth and navy beans. Bring to a boil, then reduce the heat and simmer for 40 minutes. Sprinkle with parsley and serve.

Nutrition:
• Info Per Serving: Calories: 270;Fat: 18g;Protein: 12g;-Carbs: 24g.

Arugula & Caper Green Salad

Servings:4 | Cooking Time:10 Minutes

Ingredients:
• 1 tbsp olive oil
• 10 green olives, sliced
• 4 cups baby arugula
• 1 tbsp capers, drained
• 1 tbsp balsamic vinegar
• 1 tsp lemon zest, grated
• 1 tbsp lemon juice
• 1 tsp parsley, chopped
• Salt and black pepper to taste

Directions:
1. Mix capers, olives, vinegar, lemon zest, lemon juice, oil, parsley, salt, pepper, and arugula in a bowl. Serve.

Nutrition:
• Info Per Serving: Calories: 160;Fat: 4g;Protein: 5g;-Carbs: 4g.

Kale & Bean Soup With Chorizo

Servings:4 | Cooking Time:45 Minutes

Ingredients:
• ½ cup Manchego cheese, grated
• 1 cup canned Borlotti beans, drained
• 2 tbsp olive oil
• 1 lb Spanish chorizo, sliced
• 1 carrot, chopped
• 1 yellow onion, chopped
• 1 celery stalk, chopped
• 2 garlic cloves, minced
• ½ lb kale, chopped
• 4 cups chicken stock
• 1 tsp rosemary, dried
• Salt and black pepper to taste

Directions:
1. Warm the olive oil in a large pot over medium heat and cook the chorizo for 5 minutes or until the fat is rendered and the chorizo is browned. Add in onion and continue to cook for another 3 minutes until soft and translucent. Stir in garlic and let it cook for 30-40 seconds until fragrant.

Lastly, add the carrots and celery and cook for 4-5 minutes until tender.

2. Now, pour in the chicken stock, drained and washed beans, rosemary, salt, and pepper and bring to a boil. Reduce the heat to low, cover the pot and simmer for 30 minutes. Stir periodically, checking to make sure there is enough liquid. Five minutes before the end, add the kale. Adjust the seasoning. Ladle your soup into bowls and serve topped with Manchego cheese.

Nutrition:
• Info Per Serving: Calories: 580;Fat: 27g;Protein: 27g;-Carbs: 38g.

Parmesan Roasted Red Potatoes

Servings:2 | Cooking Time: 55 Minutes

Ingredients:
• 12 ounces red potatoes, scrubbed and diced into 1-inch pieces
• 1 tablespoon olive oil
• ½ teaspoon garlic powder
• ¼ teaspoon salt
• 1 tablespoon grated Parmesan cheese
• 1 teaspoon minced fresh rosemary

Directions:
1. Preheat the oven to 425ºF. Line a baking sheet with parchment paper.
2. In a mixing bowl, combine the potatoes, olive oil, garlic powder, and salt. Toss well to coat.
3. Lay the potatoes on the parchment paper and roast for 10 minutes. Flip the potatoes over and roast for another 10 minutes.
4. Check the potatoes to make sure they are golden brown on the top and bottom. Toss them again, turn the heat down to 350ºF, and roast for 30 minutes more.
5. When the potatoes are golden brown, scatter the Parmesan cheese over them and toss again. Return to the oven for 3 minutes to melt the cheese.
6. Remove from the oven and sprinkle with the fresh rosemary before serving.

Nutrition:
• Info Per Serving: Calories: 200;Fat: 8.2g;Protein: 5.1g;-Carbs: 30.0g.

Pork & Mushroom Stew

Servings:2 | Cooking Time:50 Minutes

Ingredients:
• 2 pork chops, bones removed and cut into pieces
• 1 cup crimini mushrooms, chopped
• 2 large carrots, chopped
• ½ tsp garlic powder
• Salt and black pepper to taste
• 2 tbsp butter
• 1 cup beef broth
• 1 tbsp apple cider vinegar
• 2 tbsp cornstarch

Directions:
1. Preheat your Instant Pot on Sauté mode. Season the meat with salt and pepper. Add butter and pork chops to the pot and brown for 10 minutes, stirring occasionally. Add mushrooms and cook for 5 minutes. Add the remaining ingredients and seal the lid. Cook on High Pressure for 25 minutes. Do a quick release and serve hot.

Nutrition:
• Info Per Serving: Calories: 451;Fat: 32g;Protein: 22g;-Carbs: 17g.

Cucumber & Tomato Salad With Anchovies

Servings:4 | Cooking Time:10 Minutes

Ingredients:
• 2 tbsp extra virgin olive oil
• 1 tbsp lemon juice
• 4 canned anchovy fillets
• 6 black olives
• ½ head Romaine lettuce, torn
• Salt and black pepper to taste
• 1 cucumber, cubed
• 3 tomatoes, cubed
• 2 spring onions, chopped

Directions:
1. Whisk the olive oil, lemon juice, salt, and pepper in a bowl. Add the cucumber, tomatoes, and spring onions and toss to coat. Top with anchovies and black olives and serve.

Nutrition:
• Info Per Serving: Calories: 113;Fat: 8.5g;Protein: 2.9g;-Carbs: 9g.

Winter Cavolo Nero & Bean Soup

Servings:4 | Cooking Time:30 Minutes

Ingredients:
- 2 tbsp olive oil
- 1 onion, chopped
- 2 cloves garlic, minced
- 10 oz cavolo nero, torn
- 8 oz stelline pasta
- 6 cups vegetable broth
- 2 cups diced canned tomatoes
- 1 cup canned white beans
- Salt and black pepper to taste
- 2 tbsp Parmesan, grated

Directions:
1. Warm the olive oil in a large soup pot over medium heat. Add the onions and cook for 5 minutes, or until soft and translucent. Add the garlic and cook for 1 more minute. Pour in the broth and bring to boil. Lower the heat to low, add the tomatoes, pasta, and beans, and simmer for 5 minutes. Add the cavolo nero and stir. Cook for another 5 minutes. Season with salt and pepper. To serve, ladle into bowls and sprinkle with grated Parmesan cheese.

Nutrition:
- Info Per Serving: Calories: 388;Fat: 11g;Protein: 6g;-Carbs: 38g.

Bell Pepper & Chickpea Salad

Servings:4 | Cooking Time:40 Min + Chilling Time

Ingredients:
- 1 cup chickpeas, soaked
- 1 cucumber, sliced
- 10 cherry tomatoes, halved
- 1 red bell peppers, sliced
- 1 green bell pepper, sliced
- 1 tsp yellow mustard
- 1 tsp coriander seeds
- ½ hot banana pepper, minced
- 1 tbsp fresh lemon juice
- 1 tbsp balsamic vinegar
- 2 tbsp olive oil
- Salt and black pepper to taste
- 2 tbsp fresh cilantro, chopped
- 2 tbsp capers

Directions:
1. Cover the chickpeas with water by 2 inches in a pot over medium heat. Bring it to a boil. Turn the heat to a simmer and continue to cook for about 40 minutes or until tender. Drain, let cool and transfer to a salad bowl. Add in the remaining ingredients and toss to combine well. Serve.

Nutrition:
- Info Per Serving: Calories: 470;Fat: 13g;Protein: 22g;-Carbs: 73g.

Eggplant & Sweet Potato Salad

Servings:4 | Cooking Time:25 Minutes

Ingredients:
- 1 tbsp olive oil
- 4 cups arugula
- 2 baby eggplants, cubed
- 2 sweet potatoes, cubed
- 1 red onion, cut into wedges
- 1 tsp hot paprika
- 2 tsp cumin, ground
- Salt and black pepper to taste
- ¼ cup lime juice

Directions:
1. Warm the olive oil in a skillet over medium heat and cook eggplants and potatoes for 5 minutes. Stir in onion, paprika, cumin, salt, pepper, and lime juice and cook for another 10 minutes. Mix in arugula and serve.

Nutrition:
- Info Per Serving: Calories: 210;Fat: 9g;Protein: 5g;-Carbs: 13g.

Three-bean Salad With Black Olives

Servings:6 | Cooking Time:15 Minutes

Ingredients:
- 1 lb green beans, trimmed
- 1 red onion, thinly sliced
- 2 tbsp marjoram, chopped
- ¼ cup black olives, chopped
- ½ cup canned cannellini beans
- ½ cup canned chickpeas
- 2 tbsp extra-virgin olive oil
- ½ cup balsamic vinegar
- ½ tsp dried oregano
- Salt and black pepper to taste

Directions:
1. Steam the green beans for about 2 minutes or until just tender. Drain and place them in an ice-water bath. Drain thoroughly and pat them dry with paper towels. Put them in a large bowl and toss with the remaining ingredients. Serve.

Nutrition:
- Info Per Serving: Calories: 187;Fat: 6g;Protein: 7g;-Carbs: 27g.

Simple Mushroom Barley Soup

Servings:6 | Cooking Time: 20 To 23 Minutes

Ingredients:

- 2 tablespoons extra-virgin olive oil
- 1 cup chopped carrots
- 1 cup chopped onion
- 5½ cups chopped mushrooms
- 6 cups no-salt-added vegetable broth
- 1 cup uncooked pearled barley
- ¼ cup red wine
- 2 tablespoons tomato paste
- 4 sprigs fresh thyme or ½ teaspoon dried thyme
- 1 dried bay leaf
- 6 tablespoons grated Parmesan cheese

Directions:

1. In a large stockpot over medium heat, heat the oil. Add the onion and carrots and cook for 5 minutes, stirring frequently. Turn up the heat to medium-high and add the mushrooms. Cook for 3 minutes, stirring frequently.
2. Add the broth, barley, wine, tomato paste, thyme, and bay leaf. Stir, cover, and bring the soup to a boil. Once it's boiling, stir a few times, reduce the heat to medium-low, cover, and cook for another 12 to 15 minutes, until the barley is cooked through.
3. Remove the bay leaf and serve the soup in bowls with 1 tablespoon of cheese sprinkled on top of each.

Nutrition:

- Info Per Serving: Calories: 195;Fat: 4.0g;Protein: 7.0g;-Carbs: 34.0g.

Barley, Parsley, And Pea Salad

Servings:4 | Cooking Time: 10 Minutes

Ingredients:

- 2 cups water
- 1 cup quick-cooking barley
- 1 small bunch flat-leaf parsley, chopped
- 2 cups sugar snap pea pods
- Juice of 1 lemon
- ½ small red onion, diced
- 2 tablespoons extra-virgin olive oil
- Sea salt and freshly ground pepper, to taste

Directions:

1. Pour the water in a saucepan. Bring to a boil. Add the barley to the saucepan, then put the lid on.
2. Reduce the heat to low. Simmer the barley for 10 minutes or until the liquid is absorbed, then let sit for 5 minutes.
3. Open the lid, then transfer the barley in a colander and rinse under cold running water.
4. Pour the barley in a large salad bowl and add the remaining ingredients. Toss to combine well.
5. Serve immediately.

Nutrition:

- Info Per Serving: Calories: 152;Fat: 7.4g;Protein: 3.7g;-Carbs: 19.3g.

Turkey Egg Soup With Rice

Servings:4 | Cooking Time:40 Minutes

Ingredients:

- 2 tbsp olive oil
- 1 lb turkey breasts, cubed
- ½ cup Arborio rice
- 1 onion, chopped
- 1 celery stalk, chopped
- 1 carrot, sliced
- 1 egg
- 2 tbsp yogurt
- 1 tsp dried tarragon
- 1 tsp lemon zest
- 2 tbsp fresh parsley, chopped
- Salt and black pepper to taste

Directions:

1. Heat olive oil in a pot over medium heat and sauté the onion, celery, turkey, and carrot for 6-7 minutes, stirring occasionally. Stir in the rice for 1-2 minutes, pour in 4 cups of water, and season with salt and pepper. Bring the soup to a boil. Lower the heat and simmer for 20 minutes.
2. In a bowl, beat the egg with yogurt until well combined. Remove 1 cup of the hot soup broth with a spoon and add slowly to the egg mixture, stirring constantly. Pour the whisked mixture into the pot and stir in salt, black pepper, tarragon, and lemon zest. Garnish with parsley and serve.

Nutrition:

- Info Per Serving: Calories: 303;Fat: 11g;Protein: 23g;-Carbs: 28g.

Arugula & Fruit Salad

Servings:4 | Cooking Time:5 Minutes

Ingredients:

- 6 figs, quartered
- 2 cups arugula
- 1 cup strawberries, halved
- 1 tbsp hemp seeds
- 1 cucumber, sliced
- 1 tbsp lime juice
- 1 tbsp tahini paste

Directions:

1. Spread the arugula on a serving plate. Top with strawberries, figs, and cucumber. In another bowl, whisk tahini, hemp seeds, and lime juice and pour over the salad. Serve.

Nutrition:

- Info Per Serving: Calories: 220;Fat: 5g;Protein: 4g;-Carbs: 11g.

Caprese Salad With Tuna

Servings:4 | Cooking Time:15 Minutes

Ingredients:

- 2 tbsp extra-virgin olive oil
- 2 oz tuna in water, flaked
- 3 large tomatoes, sliced
- ¼ cup basil leaves, torn
- 4 oz fresh mozzarella, sliced
- ¼ cup balsamic vinegar
- Sea salt to taste
- 10 black olives

Directions:

1. Arrange tomatoes and mozzarella slices on a serving plate. Season with salt, scatter basil all over, and drizzle with vinegar and olive oil. Top with tuna and olives and serve.

Nutrition:

- Info Per Serving: Calories: 186;Fat: 13g;Protein: 13g;- Carbs: 6.5g.

Andalusian Gazpacho

Servings:4 | Cooking Time:15 Min + Chilling Time

Ingredients:

- 1 cucumber, peeled and chopped
- ¼ cup extra-virgin olive oil
- ¼ cup bread cubes, soaked
- 3 cups tomato juice
- 6 tomatoes, chopped
- 3 garlic cloves, minced
- 2 red bell peppers, chopped
- 1 red onion, chopped
- 1 green onion, sliced
- ½ red chili pepper, sliced
- ¼ cup red wine vinegar
- ¼ cup basil leaves, torn
- Salt and black pepper to taste

Directions:

1. In a food processor, blend cucumber, soaked bread, to- matoes, garlic, red onion, bell peppers, tomato juice, olive oil, vinegar, basil, salt, and pepper until smooth. Refrig- erate for 1-2 hours. Serve topped with 7 chili pepper and green onion.

Nutrition:

- Info Per Serving: Calories: 226;Fat: 13.4g;Protein: 5g;- Carbs: 27g.

Mustard Chicken Salad With Avocado

Servings:4 | Cooking Time:10 Minutes

Ingredients:

- 1 cup cooked chicken breasts, chopped
- ½ cup marinated artichoke hearts
- 2 tbsp olive oil
- 6 sundried tomatoes, chopped
- 1 cucumber, chopped
- 6 black olives, 6 sliced
- 2 cups Iceberg lettuce, torn
- 2 tbsp parsley, chopped
- 1 avocado, peeled and cubed
- ½ cup feta cheese, crumbled
- 4 tbsp red wine vinegar
- 2 tbsp Dijon mustard
- 1 tsp basil, dried
- 1 garlic clove, minced
- 2 tsp honey
- Salt and black pepper to taste
- 3 tbsp lemon juice

Directions:

1. Combine chicken, tomatoes, artichokes, cucumber, ol- ives, lettuce, parsley, and avocado in a bowl. In a separate bowl, whisk vinegar, mustard, basil, garlic, honey, olive oil, salt, pepper, and lemon juice and pour over the salad. Mix well. Top with cheese and serve.

Nutrition:

- Info Per Serving: Calories: 340;Fat: 23g;Protein: 10g;- Carbs: 26g.

Easy Romesco Sauce

Servings:6 | Cooking Time:10 Minutes

Ingredients:

- 1 jar roasted red peppers, drained
- 1 can diced tomatoes, undrained
- 2 garlic cloves, crushed
- 2 tsp sherry vinegar
- ½ cup dry-roasted almonds
- ⅔ cup day-old bread, torn
- 1 tsp smoked paprika
- ¼ cup extra-virgin olive oil
- Salt and black pepper to taste
- 1 tsp crushed red chili flakes

Directions:

1. Place the roasted peppers, tomatoes and their juices, almonds, garlic, vinegar, smoked paprika, salt, and pepper in your food processor. Blitz the ingredients on medium speed and slowly drizzle in the olive oil with the blender running until the dip is thoroughly mixed. Add the bread and red chili flakes and blend. Serve and enjoy!

Nutrition:

- Info Per Serving: Calories: 96;Fat: 6.8g;Protein: 3.2g;- Carbs: 8.1g.

Bell Pepper, Tomato & Egg Salad

Servings:4 | Cooking Time:15 Min + Chilling Time

Ingredients:
- 4 tbsp olive oil
- 2 hard-boiled eggs, chopped
- 2 cups Greek yogurt
- 1 cup tomatoes, chopped
- 2 mixed bell peppers, sliced
- 1 yellow onion, thinly sliced
- ½ tsp fresh garlic, minced
- 10 Kalamata olives, sliced
- 3 sun-dried tomatoes, chopped
- 1 tbsp fresh lemon juice
- 1 tsp dill, chopped
- 2 tbsp fresh parsley, chopped
- Salt and black pepper to taste

Directions:
1. In a bowl, combine the bell peppers, onion, garlic, Kalamata olives, chopped tomatoes, and sun-dried tomatoes. Stir in the chopped eggs. For the dressing, combine the lemon juice, olive oil, Greek yogurt, dill, salt, and black pepper in a bowl. Pour over the salad and transfer to the fridge to chill. Serve garnished with olives and parsley.

Nutrition:
- Info Per Serving: Calories: 279;Fat: 19g;Protein: 14g;-Carbs: 14g.

Paprika Ham & Green Lentil Soup

Servings:4 | Cooking Time:30 Minutes

Ingredients:
- 2 tbsp olive oil
- ½ lb ham, cubed
- 1 onion, chopped
- 2 tsp parsley, dried
- 1 potato, chopped
- 3 garlic cloves, chopped
- Salt and black pepper to taste
- 1 carrot, chopped
- ½ tsp paprika
- ½ cup green lentils, rinsed
- 4 cups vegetable stock
- 3 tbsp tomato paste
- 2 tomatoes, chopped

Directions:
1. Warm the olive oil in a pot over medium heat and cook ham, onion, carrot, and garlic for 4 minutes. Stir in tomato paste, paprika, and tomatoes for 2-3 minutes. Pour in lentils, vegetable stock, and potato and bring to a boil. Cook for 18-20 minutes. Adjust the seasoning with salt and pepper and sprinkle with parsley. Serve warm.

Nutrition:

- Info Per Serving: Calories: 270;Fat: 12g;Protein: 15g;-Carbs: 25g.

Cabbage & Turkey Soup

Servings:4 | Cooking Time:40 Minutes

Ingredients:
- 2 tbsp olive oil
- ½ lb turkey breast, cubed
- 2 leeks, sliced
- 4 spring onions, chopped
- 2 cups green cabbage, grated
- 4 celery sticks, chopped
- 4 cups vegetable stock
- ½ tsp sweet paprika
- ½ tsp ground nutmeg
- Salt and black pepper to taste

Directions:
1. Warm the olive oil in a pot over medium heat and brown turkey for 4 minutes, stirring occasionally. Add in leeks, spring onions, and celery and cook for another minute. Stir in cabbage, vegetable stock, sweet paprika, nutmeg, salt, and pepper and bring to a boil. Cook for 30 minutes. Serve.

Nutrition:
- Info Per Serving: Calories: 320;Fat: 16g;Protein: 19g;-Carbs: 25g.

Sautéed White Beans With Rosemary

Servings:2 | Cooking Time: 12 Minutes

Ingredients:
- 1 tablespoon olive oil
- 2 garlic cloves, minced
- 1 can white cannellini beans, drained and rinsed
- 1 teaspoon minced fresh rosemary plus 1 whole fresh rosemary sprig
- ¼ teaspoon dried sage
- ½ cup low-sodium chicken stock
- Salt, to taste

Directions:
1. Heat the olive oil in a saucepan over medium-high heat.
2. Add the garlic and sauté for 30 seconds until fragrant.
3. Add the beans, minced and whole rosemary, sage, and chicken stock and bring the mixture to a boil.
4. Reduce the heat to medium and allow to simmer for 10 minutes, or until most of the liquid is evaporated. If desired, mash some of the beans with a fork to thicken them.
5. Season with salt to taste. Remove the rosemary sprig before serving.

Nutrition:
- Info Per Serving: Calories: 155;Fat: 7.0g;Protein: 6.0g;-Carbs: 17.0g.

Sautéed Kale With Olives

Servings:2 | Cooking Time: 10 Minutes

Ingredients:
- 1 bunch kale, leaves chopped and stems minced
- ½ cup celery leaves, roughly chopped, or additional parsley
- ½ bunch flat-leaf parsley, stems and leaves roughly chopped
- 4 garlic cloves, chopped
- 2 teaspoons olive oil
- ¼ cup pitted Kalamata olives, chopped
- Grated zest and juice of 1 lemon
- Salt and pepper, to taste

Directions:
1. Place the kale, celery leaves, parsley, and garlic in a steamer basket set over a medium saucepan. Steam over medium-high heat, covered, for 15 minutes. Remove from the heat and squeeze out any excess moisture.
2. Place a large skillet over medium heat. Add the oil, then add the kale mixture to the skillet. Cook, stirring often, for 5 minutes.
3. Remove from the heat and add the olives and lemon zest and juice. Season with salt and pepper and serve.

Nutrition:
- Info Per Serving: Calories: 86;Fat: 6.4g;Protein: 1.8g;-Carbs: 7.5g.

Classic Zuppa Toscana

Servings:4 | Cooking Time:25 Minutes

Ingredients:
- 2 tbsp olive oil
- 1 yellow onion, chopped
- 4 garlic cloves, minced
- 1 celery stalk, chopped
- 1 carrot, chopped
- 15 oz canned tomatoes, diced
- 1 zucchini, chopped
- 6 cups vegetable stock
- 2 tbsp tomato paste
- 15 oz canned white beans
- 5 oz Tuscan kale
- 1 tbsp basil, chopped
- Salt and black pepper to taste

Directions:
1. Warm the olive oil in a pot over medium heat. Cook garlic and onion for 3 minutes. Stir in celery, carrot, tomatoes, zucchini, stock, tomato paste, white beans, kale, salt, and pepper and bring to a simmer. Cook for 10 minutes. Top with basil.

Nutrition:
- Info Per Serving: Calories: 480;Fat: 9g;Protein: 28g;-Carbs: 77g.

Beans , Grains, And Pastas

Beans , Grains, And Pastas

Black-Eyed Pea And Vegetable Stew

Servings:2 | Cooking Time: 40 Minutes

Ingredients:
- ½ cup black-eyed peas, soaked in water overnight
- 3 cups water, plus more as needed
- 1 large carrot, peeled and cut into ½-inch pieces (about ¾ cup)
- 1 large beet, peeled and cut into ½-inch pieces (about ¾ cup)
- ¼ teaspoon turmeric
- ¼ teaspoon cayenne pepper
- ¼ teaspoon ground cumin seeds, toasted
- ¼ cup finely chopped parsley
- ¼ teaspoon salt (optional)
- ½ teaspoon fresh lime juice

Directions:
1. Pour the black-eyed peas and water into a large pot, then cook over medium heat for 25 minutes.
2. Add the carrot and beet to the pot and cook for 10 minutes more, adding more water as needed.
3. Add the turmeric, cayenne pepper, cumin, and parsley to the pot and cook for another 6 minutes, or until the vegetables are softened. Stir the mixture periodically. Season with salt, if desired.
4. Serve drizzled with the fresh lime juice.

Nutrition:
- Info Per Serving: Calories: 89;Fat: 0.7g;Protein: 4.1g;-Carbs: 16.6g.

Creamy Saffron Chicken With Ziti

Servings:4 | Cooking Time:35 Minutes

Ingredients:
- 3 tbsp butter
- 16 oz ziti
- 4 chicken breasts, cut into strips
- ½ tsp ground saffron threads
- 1 yellow onion, chopped
- 2 garlic cloves, minced
- 1 tbsp almond flour
- 1 pinch cardamom powder
- 1 pinch cinnamon powder
- 1 cup heavy cream
- 1 cup chicken stock
- ¼ cup chopped scallions
- 3 tbsp chopped parsley
- Salt and black pepper to taste

Directions:
1. In a pot of boiling water, cook the ziti pasta for 8-10 minutes until al dente. Drain and set aside.
2. Melt the butter in a large skillet, season the chicken with salt, black pepper, and cook in the oil until golden brown on the outside, 5 minutes. Stir in the saffron, onion, garlic and cook until the onion softens and the garlic and saffron are fragrant, 3 minutes. Stir in the almond flour, cardamom powder, and cinnamon powder, and cook for 1 minute to exude some fragrance. Add the heavy cream, chicken stock and cook for 2 to 3 minutes. Adjust the taste with salt, pepper and mix in the ziti and scallions. Allow warming for 1-2 minutes and turn the heat off. Garnish with parsley.

Nutrition:
- Info Per Serving: Calories: 775;Fat: 48g;Protein: 73g;-Carbs: 3g.

Mustard Vegetable Millet

Servings:6 | Cooking Time:35 Minutes

Ingredients:
- 6 oz okra, cut into 1-inch lengths
- 3 tbsp olive oil
- 6 oz asparagus, chopped
- Salt and black pepper to taste
- 1 ½ cups whole millet
- 2 tbsp lemon juice
- 2 tbsp minced shallot
- 1 tsp Dijon mustard
- 6 oz cherry tomatoes, halved
- 3 tbsp chopped fresh dill
- 2 oz goat cheese, crumbled

Directions:
1. In a large pot, bring 4 quarts of water to a boil. Add asparagus, snap peas, and salt and cook until crisp-tender, about 3 minutes. Using a slotted spoon, transfer vegetables to a large plate and let cool completely, about 15 minutes. Add millet to water, return to a boil, and cook until grains are tender, 15-20 minutes.
2. Drain millet, spread in rimmed baking sheet, and let cool completely, 15 minutes. Whisk oil, lemon juice, shallot, mustard, salt, and pepper in a large bowl. Add vegetables, millet, tomatoes, dill, and half of the goat cheese and toss gently to combine. Season with salt and pepper. Sprinkle with remaining goat cheese to serve.

Nutrition:
- Info Per Serving: Calories: 315;Fat: 19g;Protein: 13g;-Carbs: 35g.

Simple Green Rice

Servings:4 | Cooking Time:35 Minutes

Ingredients:

- 2 tbsp butter
- 4 spring onions, sliced
- 1 leek, sliced
- 1 medium zucchini, chopped
- 5 oz broccoli florets
- 2 oz curly kale
- ½ cup frozen green peas
- 2 cloves garlic, minced
- 1 thyme sprig, chopped
- 1 rosemary sprig, chopped
- 1 cup white rice
- 2 cups vegetable broth
- 1 large tomato, chopped
- 2 oz Kalamata olives, sliced

Directions:

1. Melt the butter in a saucepan over medium heat. Cook the spring onions, leek, and zucchini for about 4-5 minutes or until tender. Add in the garlic, thyme, and rosemary and continue to sauté for about 1 minute or until aromatic. Add in the rice, broth, and tomato. Bring to a boil, turn the heat to a gentle simmer, and cook for about 10-12 minutes. Stir in broccoli, kale, and green peas, and continue cooking for 5 minutes. Fluff the rice with a fork and garnish with olives.

Nutrition:

- Info Per Serving: Calories: 403;Fat: 11g;Protein: 9g;-Carbs: 64g.

Milanese-style Risotto

Servings:4 | Cooking Time:10 Minutes

Ingredients:

- 2 tbsp olive oil
- 2 tbsp butter, softened
- 1 cup Arborio rice, cooked
- ½ cup white wine
- 1 onion, chopped
- Salt and black pepper to taste
- 2 cups hot chicken stock
- 1 pinch of saffron, soaked
- ½ cup Parmesan, grated

Directions:

1. Warm the olive oil in a skillet over medium heat and sauté onion for 3 minutes. Stir in rice, salt, and pepper for 1 minute. Pour in white wine and saffron and stir to deglaze the bottom of the skillet. Gradually add in the chicken stock while stirring; cook for 15-18 minutes. Turn off the heat and mix in butter and Parmesan cheese. Serve immediately.

Nutrition:

- Info Per Serving: Calories: 250;Fat: 10g;Protein: 5g;-Carbs: 18g.

Roasted Ratatouille Pasta

Servings:2 | Cooking Time: 30 Minutes

Ingredients:

- 1 small eggplant
- 1 small zucchini
- 1 portobello mushroom
- 1 Roma tomato, halved
- ½ medium sweet red pepper, seeded
- ½ teaspoon salt, plus additional for the pasta water
- 1 teaspoon Italian herb seasoning
- 1 tablespoon olive oil
- 2 cups farfalle pasta
- 2 tablespoons minced sun-dried tomatoes in olive oil with herbs
- 2 tablespoons prepared pesto

Directions:

1. Slice the ends off the eggplant and zucchini. Cut them lengthwise into ½-inch slices.
2. Place the eggplant, zucchini, mushroom, tomato, and red pepper in a large bowl and sprinkle with ½ teaspoon of salt. Using your hands, toss the vegetables well so that they're covered evenly with the salt. Let them rest for about 10 minutes.
3. While the vegetables are resting, preheat the oven to 400ºF. Line a baking sheet with parchment paper.
4. When the oven is hot, drain off any liquid from the vegetables and pat them dry with a paper towel. Add the Italian herb seasoning and olive oil to the vegetables and toss well to coat both sides.
5. Lay the vegetables out in a single layer on the baking sheet. Roast them for 15 to 20 minutes, flipping them over after about 10 minutes or once they start to brown on the underside. When the vegetables are charred in spots, remove them from the oven.
6. While the vegetables are roasting, fill a large saucepan with water. Add salt and cook the pasta until al dente, about 8 to 10 minutes. Drain the pasta, reserving ½ cup of the pasta water.
7. When cool enough to handle, cut the vegetables into large chunks and add them to the hot pasta.
8. Stir in the sun-dried tomatoes and pesto and toss everything well. Serve immediately.

Nutrition:

- Info Per Serving: Calories: 613;Fat: 16.0g;Protein: 23.1g;Carbs: 108.5g.

Spicy Bean Rolls

Servings:4 | Cooking Time:25 Minutes

Ingredients:
- 1 tbsp olive oil
- 1 red onion, chopped
- 2 garlic cloves, minced
- 1 green bell pepper, sliced
- 2 cups canned cannellini beans
- 1 red chili pepper, chopped
- 1 tbsp cilantro, chopped
- 1 tsp cumin, ground
- Salt and black pepper to taste
- 4 whole-wheat tortillas
- 1 cup mozzarella, shredded

Directions:

1. Warm the olive oil in a skillet over medium heat and sauté onion for 3 minutes. Stir in garlic, bell pepper, cannellini beans, red chili pepper, cilantro, cumin, salt, and pepper and cook for 15 minutes. Spoon bean mixture on each tortilla and top with cheese. Roll up and serve right away.

Nutrition:
- Info Per Serving: Calories: 680;Fat: 15g;Protein: 38g;-Carbs: 75g.

Florentine Bean & Vegetable Gratin

Servings:4 | Cooking Time:50 Minutes

Ingredients:
- ½ cup Parmigiano Reggiano cheese, grated
- 4 pancetta slices
- 2 tbsp olive oil
- 4 garlic cloves, minced
- 1 onion, chopped
- ½ fennel bulb, chopped
- 1 tbsp brown rice flour
- 2 cans white beans
- 1 can tomatoes, diced
- 1 medium zucchini, chopped
- 1 tsp porcini powder
- 1 tbsp fresh basil, chopped
- ½ tsp dried oregano
- 1 tsp red pepper flakes
- Salt to taste
- 2 tbsp butter, cubed

Directions:

1. Heat the olive in a skillet over medium heat. Fry the pancetta for 5 minutes until crispy. Drain on paper towels, chop, and reserve. Add garlic, onion, and fennel to the skillet and sauté for 5 minutes until softened. Stir in rice flour for 3 minutes.

2. Preheat oven to 350° F. Add the beans, tomatoes, and zucchini to a casserole dish and pour in the sautéed vegetable and chopped pancetta; mix well. Sprinkle with porcini powder, oregano, red pepper flakes, and salt. Top with Parmigiano Reggiano cheese and butter and bake for 25 minutes or until the cheese is lightly browned. Garnish with basil and serve.

Nutrition:
- Info Per Serving: Calories: 483;Fat: 28g;Protein: 19g;-Carbs: 42g.

Pesto Fusilli With Broccoli

Servings:4 | Cooking Time:25 Minutes

Ingredients:
- ¼ cup olive oil
- 4 Roma tomatoes, diced
- 1 cup broccoli florets
- 1 lb fusilli
- 2 tsp tomato paste
- 2 garlic cloves, minced
- 1 tbsp chopped fresh oregano
- ½ tsp salt
- 1 cup vegetable broth
- 6 fresh basil leaves
- ¼ cup grated Parmesan cheese
- ¼ cup pine nuts

Directions:

1. Place the pasta in a pot with salted boiling water and cook for 8-10 minutes until al dente. Drain and set aside. In a pan over medium heat, sauté tomato paste, tomatoes, broth, oregano, garlic, and salt for 10 minutes.

2. In a food processor, place basil, broccoli, Parmesan, olive oil, and pine nuts; pulse until smooth. Pour into the tomato mixture. Stir in pasta, cook until heated through and the pasta is well coated. Serve.

Nutrition:
- Info Per Serving: Calories: 385;Fat: 22g;Protein: 12g;-Carbs: 38g.

Israeli Style Eggplant And Chickpea Salad

Servings:6 | Cooking Time: 20 Minutes

Ingredients:
- 2 tablespoons balsamic vinegar
- 2 tablespoons freshly squeezed lemon juice
- 1 teaspoon ground cumin
- ¼ teaspoon sea salt
- 2 tablespoons olive oil, divided
- 1 medium globe eggplant, stem removed, cut into flat cubes (about ½ inch thick)
- 1 can chickpeas, drained and rinsed
- ¼ cup chopped mint leaves
- 1 cup sliced sweet onion
- 1 garlic clove, finely minced
- 1 tablespoon sesame seeds, toasted

Directions:
1. Preheat the oven to 550ºF or the highest level of your oven or broiler. Grease a baking sheet with 1 tablespoon of olive oil.
2. Combine the balsamic vinegar, lemon juice, cumin, salt, and 1 tablespoon of olive oil in a small bowl. Stir to mix well.
3. Arrange the eggplant cubes on the baking sheet, then brush with 2 tablespoons of the balsamic vinegar mixture on both sides.
4. Broil in the preheated oven for 8 minutes or until lightly browned. Flip the cubes halfway through the cooking time.
5. Meanwhile, combine the chickpeas, mint, onion, garlic, and sesame seeds in a large serving bowl. Drizzle with remaining balsamic vinegar mixture. Stir to mix well.
6. Remove the eggplant from the oven. Allow to cool for 5 minutes, then slice them into ½-inch strips on a clean work surface.
7. Add the eggplant strips in the serving bowl, then toss to combine well before serving.

Nutrition:
- Info Per Serving: Calories: 125;Fat: 2.9g;Protein: 5.2g;-Carbs: 20.9g.

Apricot & Almond Couscous

Servings:4 | Cooking Time:25 Minutes

Ingredients:
- 2 tbsp olive oil
- 1 small onion, diced
- 1 cup couscous
- 2 cups water
- ½ cup dried apricots, soaked
- ½ cup slivered hazelnuts
- ½ tsp dried mint
- ½ tsp dried thyme

Directions:
1. In a skillet, heat the olive and stir-fry the onion until translucent and soft. Stir in the couscous and cook for 2-3 minutes. Add the water, cover, and cook for 8-10 minutes until the water is mostly absorbed. Remove from the heat and let sit for a few minutes. Fluff with a fork and fold in the apricots, nuts, mint, and thyme.

Nutrition:
- Info Per Serving: Calories: 388;Fat: 8g;Protein: 14g;-Carbs: 36g.

Valencian-Style Mussel Rice

Servings:4 | Cooking Time:40 Minutes

Ingredients:
- 1 lb mussels, cleaned and debearded
- 2 tbsp olive oil
- 2 garlic cloves, minced
- 1 yellow onion, chopped
- 2 tomatoes, chopped
- 2 cups fish stock
- 1 cup white rice
- 1 bunch parsley, chopped
- Salt and white pepper to taste

Directions:
1. Warm the olive oil in a pot over medium heat and cook onion and garlic for 5 minutes. Stir in rice for 1 minute. Pour in tomatoes and fish stock and bring to a boil. Add in the mussels and simmer for 20 minutes. Discard any unopened mussels. Adjust the taste with salt and white pepper. Serve topped with parsley.

Nutrition:
- Info Per Serving: Calories: 310;Fat: 15g;Protein: 12g;-Carbs: 17g.

Spinach & Salmon Fettuccine In White Sauce

Servings:4 | Cooking Time:35 Minutes

Ingredients:
- 5 tbsp butter
- 16 oz fettuccine
- 4 salmon fillets, cubed
- Salt and black pepper to taste
- 3 garlic cloves, minced
- 1 ¼ cups heavy cream
- ½ cup dry white wine
- 1 tsp grated lemon zest
- 1 cup baby spinach
- Lemon wedges for garnishing

Directions:
1. In a pot of boiling water, cook the fettuccine pasta for

8-10 minutes until al dente. Drain and set aside.

2. Melt half of the butter in a large skillet; season the salmon with salt, black pepper, and cook in the butter until golden brown on all sides and flaky within, 8 minutes. Transfer to a plate and set aside.

3. Add the remaining butter to the skillet to melt and stir in the garlic. Cook until fragrant, 1 minute. Mix in heavy cream, white wine, lemon zest, salt, and pepper. Allow boiling over low heat for 5 minutes. Stir in spinach, allow wilting for 2 minutes and stir in fettuccine and salmon until well-coated in the sauce. Garnish with lemon wedges.

Nutrition:
• Info Per Serving: Calories: 795;Fat: 46g;Protein: 72g;-Carbs: 20g.

Arrabbiata Penne Rigate

Servings:4 | Cooking Time:30 Minutes

Ingredients:
• 2 tbsp olive oil
• 1 onion, chopped
• 6 cloves garlic, minced
• ½ red chili, chopped
• 2 cups canned tomatoes, diced
• ½ tsp sugar
• Salt and black pepper to taste
• 1 lb penne rigate
• 1 cup shredded mozzarella
• 1 cup fresh basil, chopped
• ½ cup grated Parmesan cheese

Directions:
1. Bring a large pot of salted water to a boil, add the penne, and cook for 7-9 minutes until al dente. Reserve ¼ cup pasta cooking water and drain pasta. Set aside.
2. Warm the oil in a saucepan over medium heat. Sauté the onion and garlic for 3-5 minutes or until softened. Add tomatoes with their liquid, black pepper, sugar, and salt. Cook 20 minutes or until the sauce thickens. Add the pasta and reserved cooking water and stir for 2-3 minutes. Add mozzarella cheese and red chili and cook until the cheese melts, 3-4 minutes. Top with Parmesan and basil and serve.

Nutrition:
• Info Per Serving: Calories: 454;Fat: 12g;Protein: 18g;-Carbs: 70g.

Mashed Beans With Cumin

Servings:4 | Cooking Time: 10 To 12 Minutes

Ingredients:
• 1 tablespoon extra-virgin olive oil, plus extra for serving
• 4 garlic cloves, minced
• 1 teaspoon ground cumin
• 2 cans fava beans
• 3 tablespoons tahini
• 2 tablespoons lemon juice, plus lemon wedges for serving
• Salt and pepper, to taste
• 1 tomato, cored and cut into ½-inch pieces
• 1 small onion, chopped finely
• 2 hard-cooked large eggs, chopped
• 2 tablespoons minced fresh parsley

Directions:
1. Add the olive oil, garlic and cumin to a medium saucepan over medium heat. Cook for about 2 minutes, or until fragrant.
2. Stir in the beans with their liquid and tahini. Bring to a simmer and cook for 8 to 10 minutes, or until the liquid thickens slightly.
3. Turn off the heat, mash the beans to a coarse consistency with a potato masher. Stir in the lemon juice and 1 teaspoon pepper. Season with salt and pepper.
4. Transfer the mashed beans to a serving dish. Top with the tomato, onion, eggs and parsley. Drizzle with the extra olive oil.
5. Serve with the lemon wedges.

Nutrition:
• Info Per Serving: Calories: 125;Fat: 8.6g;Protein: 4.9g;-Carbs: 9.1g.

Swoodles With Almond Butter Sauce

Servings:4 | Cooking Time: 20 Minutes

Ingredients:
• Sauce:
• 1 garlic clove
• 1-inch piece fresh ginger, peeled and sliced
• ¼ cup chopped yellow onion
• ¾ cup almond butter
• 1 tablespoon tamari
• 1 tablespoon raw honey
• 1 teaspoon paprika
• 1 tablespoon fresh lemon juice
• ⅛ teaspoon ground red pepper
• Sea salt and ground black pepper, to taste
• ¼ cup water
• Swoodles:
• 2 large sweet potatoes, spiralized
• 2 tablespoons coconut oil, melted
• Sea salt and ground black pepper, to taste
• For Serving:
• ½ cup fresh parsley, chopped
• ½ cup thinly sliced scallions

Directions:
1. Make the Sauce
2. Put the garlic, ginger, and onion in a food processor,

then pulse to combine well.

3. Add the almond butter, tamari, honey, paprika, lemon juice, ground red pepper, salt, and black pepper to the food processor. Pulse to combine well. Pour in the water during the pulsing until the mixture is thick and smooth.

4. Make the Swoodles:

5. Preheat the oven to 425°F. Line a baking sheet with parchment paper.

6. Put the spiralized sweet potato in a bowl, then drizzle with olive oil. Toss to coat well. Transfer them on the baking sheet. Sprinkle with salt and pepper.

7. Bake in the preheated oven for 20 minutes or until lightly browned and al dente. Check the doneness during the baking and remove any well-cooked swoodles.

8. Transfer the swoodles on a large plate and spread with sauce, parsley, and scallions. Toss to serve.

Nutrition:
• Info Per Serving: Calories: 441;Fat: 33.6g;Protein: 12.0g;Carbs: 29.6g.

Basic Brown Rice Pilaf With Capers

Servings:4 | Cooking Time:30 Minutes

Ingredients:
• 2 tbsp olive oil
• 1 cup brown rice
• 1 onion, chopped
• 1 celery stalk, chopped
• 2 garlic cloves, minced
• ½ cup capers, rinsed
• Salt and black pepper to taste
• 2 tbsp parsley, chopped

Directions:
1. Warm the olive oil in a skillet over medium heat. Sauté celery, garlic, and onion for 10 minutes. Stir in rice, capers, 2 cups of water, salt, and pepper and cook for 25 minutes. Serve topped with parsley.

Nutrition:
• Info Per Serving: Calories: 230;Fat: 8.9g;Protein: 7g;-Carbs: 16g.

Moroccan-style Vegetable Bean Stew

Servings:6 | Cooking Time:50 Minutes

Ingredients:
• 3 tbsp olive oil
• 1 onion, chopped
• 8 oz Swiss chard, torn
• 4 garlic cloves, minced
• 1 tsp ground cumin
• ½ tsp paprika
• ½ tsp ground coriander
• ¼ tsp ground cinnamon
• 2 tbsp tomato paste
• 2 tbsp cornstarch
• 4 cups vegetable broth
• 2 carrots, chopped
• 1 can chickpeas
• 1 can butter beans
• 3 tbsp minced fresh parsley
• 3 tbsp harissa sauce
• Salt and black pepper to taste

Directions:
1. Warm the olive oil in a saucepan over medium heat. Sauté the onion until softened, about 3 minutes. Stir in garlic, cumin, paprika, coriander, and cinnamon and cook until fragrant, about 30 seconds. Stir in tomato paste and cornstarch and cook for 1 minute. Pour in broth and carrots, scraping up any browned bits, smoothing out any lumps, and bringing to boil. Reduce to a gentle simmer and cook for 10 minutes. Stir in chard, chickpeas, beans, salt, and pepper and simmer until vegetables are tender, 10-15 minutes. Sprinkle with parsley and some harissa sauce. Serve with the remaining sauce harissa on the side.

Nutrition:
• Info Per Serving: Calories: 387;Fat: 3.2g;Protein: 7g;-Carbs: 28.7g.

Freekeh Pilaf With Dates And Pistachios

Servings:4 | Cooking Time: 10 Minutes

Ingredients:
• 2 tablespoons extra-virgin olive oil, plus extra for drizzling
• 1 shallot, minced
• 1½ teaspoons grated fresh ginger
• ¼ teaspoon ground coriander
• ¼ teaspoon ground cumin
• Salt and pepper, to taste
• 1¾ cups water
• 1½ cups cracked freekeh, rinsed
• 3 ounces pitted dates, chopped
• ¼ cup shelled pistachios, toasted and coarsely chopped
• 1½ tablespoons lemon juice
• ¼ cup chopped fresh mint

Directions:
1. Set the Instant Pot to Sauté mode and heat the olive oil until shimmering.

2. Add the shallot, ginger, coriander, cumin, salt, and pepper to the pot and cook for about 2 minutes, or until the shallot is softened. Stir in the water and freekeh.

3. Secure the lid. Select the Manual mode and set the cooking time for 4 minutes at High Pressure. Once cooking is complete, do a quick pressure release. Carefully open the lid.

4. Add the dates, pistachios and lemon juice and gently fluff the freekeh with a fork to combine. Season to taste with salt and pepper.

5. Transfer to a serving dish and sprinkle with the mint. Serve drizzled with extra olive oil.

Nutrition:
- Info Per Serving: Calories: 280;Fat: 8.0g;Protein: 8.0g;-Carbs: 46.0g.

Carrot & Barley Risotto

Servings:6 | Cooking Time:1 Hour 20 Minutes

Ingredients:
- 2 tbsp olive oil
- 4 cups vegetable broth
- 4 cups water
- 1 onion, chopped fine
- 1 carrot, chopped
- 1 ½ cups pearl barley
- 1 cup dry white wine
- ¼ tsp dried oregano
- 2 oz Parmesan cheese, grated
- Salt and black pepper to taste

Directions:
1. Bring broth and water to a simmer in a saucepan. Reduce heat to low and cover to keep warm.
2. Heat 1 tbsp of oil in a pot over medium heat until sizzling. Stir-fry onion and carrot until softened, 6-7 minutes. Add barley and cook, stirring often, until lightly toasted and aromatic, 4 minutes. Add wine and cook, stirring frequently for 2 minutes. Stir in 3 cups of water and oregano, bring to a simmer, and cook, stirring occasionally until liquid is absorbed, 25 minutes. Stir in 2 cups of broth, bring to a simmer, and cook until the liquid is absorbed, 15 minutes.
3. Continue cooking, stirring often and adding warm broth as needed to prevent the pot bottom from becoming dry until barley is cooked through but still somewhat firm in the center, 15-20 minutes. Off heat, adjust consistency with the remaining warm broth as needed. Stir in Parmesan and the remaining oil and season with salt and pepper to taste. Serve.

Nutrition:
- Info Per Serving: Calories: 355;Fat: 21g;Protein: 16g;-Carbs: 35g.

Classic Falafel

Servings:6 | Cooking Time:20 Minutes

Ingredients:
- 2 cups olive oil
- Salt and black pepper to taste
- 1 cup chickpeas, soaked
- 5 scallions, chopped
- ¼ cup fresh parsley leaves
- ¼ cup fresh cilantro leaves
- ¼ cup fresh dill
- 6 garlic cloves, minced
- ½ tsp ground cumin
- ½ tsp ground coriander

Directions:
1. Pat dry chickpeas with paper towels and place them in your food processor. Add in scallions, parsley, cilantro, dill, garlic, salt, pepper, cumin, and ground coriander and pulse, scraping downsides of the bowl as needed. Shape the chickpea mixture into 2-tablespoon-size disks, about 1 ½ inches wide and 1 inch thick, and place on a parchment paper–lined baking sheet.
2. Warm the olive oil in a skillet over medium heat. Fry the falafel until deep golden brown, 2-3 minutes per side. With a slotted spoon, transfer falafel to a paper towel-lined plate to drain. Serve hot.

Nutrition:
- Info Per Serving: Calories: 349;Fat: 26.3g;Protein: 19g;-Carbs: 9g.

Rosemary Barley With Walnuts

Servings:4 | Cooking Time:45 Minutes

Ingredients:
- 2 tbsp olive oil
- ½ cup diced onion
- ½ cup diced celery
- 1 carrot, peeled and diced
- 3 cups water
- 1 cup barley
- ½ tsp thyme
- ½ tsp rosemary
- ¼ cup pine nuts
- Salt and black pepper to taste

Directions:
1. Warm the olive oil in a medium saucepan over medium heat. Sauté the onion, celery, and carrot over medium heat until tender. Add the water, barley, and seasonings, and bring to a boil. Reduce the heat and simmer for 23 minutes or until tender. Stir in the pine nuts and season to taste. Serve warm.

Nutrition:
- Info Per Serving: Calories: 276;Fat: 9g;Protein: 7g;-Carbs: 41g.

Spanish-Style Linguine With Tapenade

Servings:4 | Cooking Time:20 Minutes

Ingredients:
- 1 cup black olives, pitted
- 2 tbsp capers
- 2 tbsp rosemary, chopped
- 1 garlic clove, smashed
- 2 anchovy fillets, chopped
- ½ tsp sugar
- ⅔ cup + 2 tbsp olive oil
- 1 lb linguine
- ½ cup grated Manchego cheese
- 1 tbsp chopped fresh chives

Directions:
1. Process the olives, capers, rosemary, garlic, anchovies, sugar, and ⅔ cup olive oil in your food processor until well incorporated but not smooth; set aside. Bring a large pot of salted water to a boil, add the linguine, and cook for 7-9 minutes until al dente. Drain the pasta in a bowl and add the remaining 2 tablespoons olive oil and Manchego cheese; toss to coat. Arrange pasta on a serving platter and top it with tapenade and chives. Serve and enjoy!

Nutrition:
- Info Per Serving: Calories: 375;Fat: 39g;Protein: 5g;-Carbs: 23g.

Rigatoni With Peppers & Mozzarella

Servings:4 | Cooking Time:30 Min + Marinating Time

Ingredients:
- 1 lb fresh mozzarella cheese, cubed
- 3 tbsp olive oil
- ¼ cup chopped fresh chives
- ¼ cup basil, chopped
- ½ tsp red pepper flakes
- 1 tsp apple cider vinegar
- Salt and black pepper to taste
- 3 garlic cloves, minced
- 2 cups sliced onions
- 3 cups bell peppers, sliced
- 2 cups tomato sauce
- 8 oz rigatoni
- 1 tbsp butter
- ¼ cup grated Parmesan cheese

Directions:
1. Bring to a boil salted water in a pot over high heat. Add the rigatoni and cook according to package directions. Drain and set aside, reserving 1 cup of the cooking water. Combine the mozzarella, 1 tablespoon of olive oil, chives, basil, pepper flakes, apple cider vinegar, salt, and pepper. Let the cheese marinate for 30 minutes at room temperature.

2. Warm the remaining olive oil in a large skillet over medium heat. Stir-fry the garlic for 10 seconds and add the onions and peppers. Cook for 3-4 minutes, stirring occasionally until the onions are translucent. Pour in the tomato sauce, and reduce the heat to a simmer. Add the rigatoni and reserved cooking water and toss to coat. Heat off and adjust the seasoning with salt and pepper. Toss with marinated mozzarella cheese and butter. Sprinkle with Parmesan cheese and serve.

Nutrition:
- Info Per Serving: Calories: 434;Fat: 18g;Protein: 44g;-Carbs: 27g.

Caprese Pasta With Roasted Asparagus

Servings:6 | Cooking Time: 25 Minutes

Ingredients:
- 8 ounces uncooked small pasta, like orecchiette (little ears) or farfalle (bow ties)
- 1½ pounds fresh asparagus, ends trimmed and stalks chopped into 1-inch pieces
- 1½ cups grape tomatoes, halved
- 2 tablespoons extra-virgin olive oil
- ¼ teaspoon kosher salt
- ¼ teaspoon freshly ground black pepper
- 2 cups fresh Mozzarella, drained and cut into bite-size pieces
- ⅓ cup torn fresh basil leaves
- 2 tablespoons balsamic vinegar

Directions:
1. Preheat the oven to 400ºF.
2. In a large stockpot of salted water, cook the pasta for about 8 to 10 minutes. Drain and reserve about ¼ cup of the cooking liquid.
3. Meanwhile, in a large bowl, toss together the asparagus, tomatoes, oil, salt and pepper. Spread the mixture onto a large, rimmed baking sheet and bake in the oven for 15 minutes, stirring twice during cooking.
4. Remove the vegetables from the oven and add the cooked pasta to the baking sheet. Mix with a few tablespoons of cooking liquid to help the sauce become smoother and the saucy vegetables stick to the pasta.
5. Gently mix in the Mozzarella and basil. Drizzle with the balsamic vinegar. Serve from the baking sheet or pour the pasta into a large bowl.

Nutrition:
- Info Per Serving: Calories: 147;Fat: 3.0g;Protein: 16.0g;-Carbs: 17.0g.

Italian Tarragon Buckwheat

Servings:6 | Cooking Time:55 Minutes

Ingredients:
- 3 tbsp olive oil
- 1 ½ cups buckwheat, soaked
- 3 cups vegetable broth
- ½ onion, finely chopped
- 1 garlic clove, minced
- 2 tsp fresh tarragon, minced
- Salt and black pepper to taste
- 2 oz Parmesan cheese, grated
- 2 tbsp parsley, minced
- 2 tsp lemon juice

Directions:
1. Pulse buckwheat in your blender until about half of the grains are broken into smaller pieces. Bring broth and 3 cups of water to a boil in a medium saucepan over high heat. Reduce heat to low, cover, and keep warm.
2. Warm 2 tablespoons oil in a pot over medium heat. Add onion and cook until softened, 5 minutes. Stir in garlic and cook until fragrant, about 30 seconds. Add farro and cook, stirring frequently, until grains are lightly toasted, 3 minutes.
3. Stir 5 cups warm broth mixture into farro mixture, reduce heat to low, cover, and cook until almost all liquid has been absorbed and farro is just al dente, about 25 minutes, stirring twice during cooking.
4. Add tarragon, salt, and pepper and keep stirring for 5 minutes. Remove from heat and stir in Parmesan cheese, parsley, lemon juice, and the remaining olive oil. Adjust the seasoning and serve.

Nutrition:
- Info Per Serving: Calories: 321;Fat: 21g;Protein: 15g;-Carbs: 35g.

Greek-Style Shrimp & Feta Macaroni

Servings:6 | Cooking Time:50 Minutes

Ingredients:
- 10 Kalamata olives
- 1 ½ lb elbow macaroni
- 2 red chili peppers, minced
- 1 garlic clove, minced
- 2 whole garlic cloves
- 2 tbsp fresh parsley, chopped
- 1 ¼ cups fresh basil, sliced
- ½ cup extra-virgin olive oil
- ½ tsp honey
- ½ lemon, juiced and zested
- ¼ cup butter
- 1 small red onion, chopped
- 1 lb button mushrooms, sliced
- 1 tsp sweet paprika
- 6 ripe plum tomatoes, puréed
- ¼ cup dry white wine
- 1 oz ouzo
- 1 cup heavy cream
- 1 cup feta cheese, crumbled
- 24 shrimp, peeled and deveined
- 1 cup feta cheese, cubed
- 1 tsp dried Greek oregano
- Salt and black pepper to taste

Directions:
1. Bring to a boil salted water in a pot over high heat. Add the macaroni and cook for 6-8 minutes until al dente. Drain. Set aside. Preheat your broiler. Place the chilies, whole garlic, parsley, ¼ cup of basil, ¼ cup of oil, honey, lemon juice, lemon zest, and salt in a food processor and blend until all the ingredients are well incorporated. Set aside.
2. Warm the remaining olive oil and butter in a large skillet over medium heat. Sauté the onion, minced garlic, mushrooms, and paprika for 5 minutes until tender. Pour in the tomatoes, wine, and ouzo and season with salt and pepper. Simmer for 6–7 minutes until most of the liquid evaporates, 5 minutes.
3. Stir in the heavy cream and crumbled feta cheese for 3 minutes until the sauce is thickened. Add in remaining basil and pasta and stir to combine. Pour the mixture into a baking dish and top with shrimp and cubed feta cheese. Broil 5 minutes or until the shrimp turn pink and cheese melts. Drizzle with reserved parsley-basil sauce and sprinkle with oregano. Let cool for 5 minutes. Serve topped with olives.

Nutrition:
- Info Per Serving: Calories: 1004;Fat: 47g;Protein: 47g;-Carbs: 97g.

Chicken Linguine A La Toscana

Servings:4 | Cooking Time:35 Minutes

Ingredients:
- 1 cup sundried tomatoes in oil, chopped
- ¾ cup grated Pecorino Romano cheese
- 2 tbsp olive oil
- 16 oz linguine
- 4 chicken breasts
- 1 white onion, chopped
- 1 red bell pepper, chopped
- 5 garlic cloves, minced
- ¾ cup chicken broth
- 1 ½ cups heavy cream
- 1 cup baby kale, chopped
- Salt and black pepper to taste

Directions:
1. In a pot of boiling water, cook the linguine pasta for 8-10

minutes until al dente. Drain and set aside.

2. Heat the olive oil in a large skillet, season the chicken with salt, black pepper, and cook in the oil until golden brown on the outside and cooked within, 7 to 8 minutes. Transfer the chicken to a plate and cut into 4 slices each. Set aside.

3. Add the onion, sundried tomatoes, bell pepper to the skillet and sauté until softened, 5 minutes. Mix in the garlic and cook until fragrant, 1 minute. Deglaze the skillet with the chicken broth and mix in the heavy cream. Simmer for 2 minutes and stir in the Pecorino Romano cheese until melted, 2 minutes. Once the cheese melts, stir in the kale to wilt and adjust the taste with salt and black pepper. Mix in the linguine and chicken until well coated in the sauce. Dish the food and serve warm.

Nutrition:
• Info Per Serving: Calories: 941;Fat: 61g;Protein: 79g;-Carbs: 11g.

Sun-dried Tomato & Basil Risotto

Servings:4 | Cooking Time:35 Minutes

Ingredients:
• 10 oz sundried tomatoes in olive oil, drained and chopped
• 2 tbsp olive oil
• 2 cups chicken stock
• 1 onion, chopped
• 1 cup Arborio rice
• Salt and black pepper to taste
• 1 cup Pecorino cheese, grated
• ¼ cup basil leaves, chopped

Directions:
1. Warm the olive oil in a skillet over medium heat and cook onion and sundried tomatoes for 5 minutes. Stir in rice, chicken stock, salt, pepper, and basil and bring to a boil. Cook for 20 minutes. Mix in Pecorino cheese and serve.

Nutrition:
• Info Per Serving: Calories: 430;Fat: 9g;Protein: 8g;-Carbs: 57g.

Simple Lentil Risotto

Servings:2 | Cooking Time: 20 Minutes

Ingredients:
• ½ tablespoon olive oil
• ½ medium onion, chopped
• ½ cup dry lentils, soaked overnight
• ½ celery stalk, chopped
• 1 sprig parsley, chopped
• ½ cup Arborio (short-grain Italian) rice

• 1 garlic clove, lightly mashed
• 2 cups vegetable stock

Directions:
1. Press the Sauté button to heat your Instant Pot.
2. Add the oil and onion to the Instant Pot and sauté for 5 minutes.
3. Add all the remaining ingredients to the Instant Pot.
4. Secure the lid. Select the Manual mode and set the cooking time for 15 minutes at High Pressure.
5. Once cooking is complete, do a natural pressure release for 20 minutes, then release any remaining pressure. Carefully open the lid.
6. Stir and serve hot.

Nutrition:
• Info Per Serving: Calories: 261;Fat: 3.6g;Protein: 10.6g;-Carbs: 47.1g.

Authentic Fava Bean & Garbanzo Fül

Servings:6 | Cooking Time:20 Minutes

Ingredients:
• 3 tbsp extra-virgin olive oil
• 1 can garbanzo beans
• 1 can fava beans
• ½ tsp lemon zest
• ½ tsp dried oregano
• ½ cup lemon juice
• 3 cloves garlic, minced
• Salt to taste

Directions:
1. Place the garbanzo beans, fava beans, and 3 cups of water in a pot over medium heat. Cook for 10 minutes. Drain the beans Reserving 1 cup of the liquid, and put them in a bowl. Mix the reserved liquid, lemon juice, lemon zest, oregano, minced garlic, and salt together and add to the beans in the bowl. With a potato masher, mash up about half the beans in the bowl. Stir the mixture to combine. Drizzle the olive oil over the top. Serve with pita bread if desired.

Nutrition:
• Info Per Serving: Calories: 199;Fat: 9g;Protein: 10g;-Carbs: 25g.

Classic Lentil Stew With Goat Cheese

Servings:4 | Cooking Time:35 Minutes

Ingredients:
- 1 tbsp olive oil
- 1 carrot, sliced
- 1 onion, chopped
- 1 celery stalk, chopped
- 2 garlic cloves, minced
- 1 lb potatoes, cubed
- 1 cup lentils
- ½ tsp paprika
- Salt and black pepper to taste
- 14 oz canned tomatoes, diced
- 2 tbsp cilantro, chopped
- 4 oz goat cheese, sliced

Directions:
1. Warm the olive oil in a pot over medium heat and sauté onion, garlic, celery, and carrot for 5 minutes. Stir in potatoes, lentils, paprika, salt, pepper, and tomatoes. Pour in 2 cups of water and bring to a boil. Simmer for 20 minutes. Sprinkle with cilantro and top with goat cheese slices to serve.

Nutrition:
- Info Per Serving: Calories: 330;Fat: 18g;Protein: 17g;-Carbs: 27g.

Leftover Pasta & Mushroom Frittata

Servings:4 | Cooking Time:25 Minutes

Ingredients:
- 2 tbsp olive oil
- 4 oz leftover spaghetti, cooked
- 8 large eggs, beaten
- ¼ cup heavy cream
- ½ tsp Italian seasoning
- ½ tsp garlic salt
- 1/8 tsp garlic pepper
- 1 cup chopped mushrooms
- 1 cup Pecorino cheese, grated

Directions:
1. Preheat your broiler. Warm the olive oil in a large skillet over medium heat. Add mushrooms and cook for 3–4 minutes, until almost tender. In a large bowl, beat the eggs with cream, Italian seasoning, garlic salt, and garlic pepper. Stir in the leftover spaghetti. Pour the egg mixture over the mushrooms and level with a spatula. Cook for 5–7 minutes until the eggs are almost set. Sprinkle with cheese and place under broiler for 3–5 minutes, until the cheese melts. Serve.

Nutrition:
- Info Per Serving: Calories: 400;Fat: 30g;Protein: 23g;-Carbs: 11g.

Tomato Sauce And Basil Pesto Fettuccine

Servings:4 | Cooking Time: 15 Minutes

Ingredients:
- 4 Roma tomatoes, diced
- 2 teaspoons no-salt-added tomato paste
- 1 tablespoon chopped fresh oregano
- 2 garlic cloves, minced
- 1 cup low-sodium vegetable soup
- ½ teaspoon sea salt
- 1 packed cup fresh basil leaves
- ¼ cup pine nuts
- ¼ cup grated Parmesan cheese
- 2 tablespoons extra-virgin olive oil
- 1 pound cooked whole-grain fettuccine

Directions:
1. Put the tomatoes, tomato paste, oregano, garlic, vegetable soup, and salt in a skillet. Stir to mix well.
2. Cook over medium heat for 10 minutes or until lightly thickened.
3. Put the remaining ingredients, except for the fettuccine, in a food processor and pulse to combine until smooth.
4. Pour the puréed basil mixture into the tomato mixture, then add the fettuccine. Cook for a few minutes or until heated through and the fettuccine is well coated.
5. Serve immediately.

Nutrition:
- Info Per Serving: Calories: 389;Fat: 22.7g;Protein: 9.7g;-Carbs: 40.2g.

One-Pot Linguine With Brussels Sprouts

Servings:4 | Cooking Time:35 Minutes

Ingredients:
- 8 oz whole-wheat linguine
- ⅔ cup + 2 tbsp olive oil
- 1 medium sweet onion, diced
- 2 garlic cloves, minced
- 1 tsp red chili flakes
- 1 lb Brussels sprouts, shredded
- ½ cup chicken stock
- ⅔ cup dry white wine
- ½ cup grated Parmesan cheese
- 1 lemon, juiced
- 2 tbsp parsley, chopped

Directions:
1. Cook pasta in boiling salted water according to package directions. Reserve 1 cup of the pasta water. Drain the linguine and mix with 2 tablespoons of olive oil; set aside.
2. Warm the remaining olive oil in a skillet over medium heat. Sauté the onion for 3 minutes, until softened. Add the garlic and cook for 1 minute, until fragrant. Stir in the

Brussels sprouts and cook covered for 15 minutes. Pour in chicken stock and cook for 3-4 more minutes until the sprouts are fork-tender. Add white wine and cook for 5-7 minutes, until reduced. Add the pasta to the skillet and the pasta water. Serve with Parmesan cheese, chili flakes, and lemon juice.

Nutrition:
• Info Per Serving: Calories: 501;Fat: 31g;Protein: 15g;-Carbs: 49g.

Bell Pepper & Bean Salad

Servings:6 | Cooking Time:30 Minutes

Ingredients:
• ¼ cup extra-virgin olive oil
• 3 garlic cloves, minced
• 2 cans cannellini beans
• Salt and black pepper to taste
• 2 tsp sherry vinegar
• 1 red onion, sliced
• 1 red bell pepper, chopped
• ¼ cup chopped fresh parsley
• 2 tsp chopped fresh chives
• ¼ tsp crushed red pepper

Directions:
1. Warm 1 tbsp of olive oil in a saucepan over medium heat. Sauté the garlic until it turns golden but not brown, about 3 minutes. Add beans, 2 cups of water, and salt, and pepper, and bring to a simmer. Heat off. Let sit for 20 minutes.
2. Mix well the vinegar and red onion in a salad bowl. Drain the beans and remove the garlic. Add beans, remaining olive oil, bell pepper, parsley, crushed red pepper, chives, salt, and pepper to the onion mixture and gently toss to combine.

Nutrition:
• Info Per Serving: Calories: 131;Fat: 7.7g;Protein: 6g;-Carbs: 13.5g.

Chili Pork Rice

Servings:4 | Cooking Time:8 Hours 10 Minutes

Ingredients:
• 3 tbsp olive oil
• 2 lb pork loin, sliced
• 1 cup chicken stock
• ½ tbsp chili powder
• 2 tsp thyme, dried
• ½ tbsp garlic powder
• Salt and black pepper to taste
• 2 cups rice, cooked

Directions:

1. Place pork, chicken stock, oil, chili powder, garlic powder, salt, and pepper in your slow cooker. Cover with the lid and cook for 8 hours on Low. Share pork into plates with a side of rice and garnish with thyme to serve.

Nutrition:
• Info Per Serving: Calories: 280;Fat: 15g;Protein: 15g;-Carbs: 17g.

Traditional Beef Lasagna

Servings:4 | Cooking Time:70 Minutes

Ingredients:
• 2 tbsp olive oil
• 1 lb lasagne sheets
• 1 lb ground beef
• 1 white onion, chopped
• 1 tsp Italian seasoning
• Salt and black pepper to taste
• 1 cup marinara sauce
• ½ cup grated Parmesan cheese

Directions:
1. Preheat oven to 350° F. Warm olive oil in a skillet and add the beef and onion. Cook until the beef is brown, 7-8 minutes. Season with Italian seasoning, salt, and pepper. Cook for 1 minute and mix in the marinara sauce. Simmer for 3 minutes.
2. Spread a layer of the beef mixture in a lightly greased baking sheet and make a first single layer on the beef mixture. Top with a single layer of lasagna sheets. Repeat the layering two more times using the remaining ingredients in the same quantities. Sprinkle with Parmesan cheese. Bake in the oven until the cheese melts and is bubbly with the sauce, 20 minutes. Remove the lasagna, allow cooling for 2 minutes and dish onto serving plates. Serve warm.

Nutrition:
• Info Per Serving: Calories: 557;Fat: 29g;Protein: 60g;-Carbs: 4g.

Vegetable Lentils With Brown Rice

Servings:4 | Cooking Time:40 Minutes

Ingredients:
• 1 ½ tbsp olive oil
• 2 ¼ cups vegetable broth
• ½ cup green lentils
• ½ cup brown rice
• ½ cup diced carrots
• ½ cup diced celery
• 1 can sliced olives
• ¼ cup diced red onion
• ¼ cup cilantro, chopped
• 1 tbsp lemon juice

- 1 garlic clove, minced
- Salt and black pepper to taste

Directions:

1. In a saucepan over high heat, bring the broth and lentils to a boil, cover, and lower the heat to medium-low. Cook for 8 minutes. Raise the heat to medium, and stir in the rice. Cover the pot and cook the mixture for 14 minutes or until the liquid is absorbed. Remove the pot from the heat and let sit covered for 2 minutes, then stir.

2. While the lentils and rice are cooking, combine carrots, celery, olives, onion, and cilantro in a serving bowl. In a small bowl, whisk together the oil, lemon juice, garlic, salt, and black pepper. Set aside. Once the lentils and rice are done, add them to the serving bowl. Pour the dressing on top, and mix well. Serve warm.

Nutrition:
- Info Per Serving: Calories: 203;Fat: 7g;Protein: 10g;-Carbs: 33g.

Stewed Borlotti Beans

Servings:6 | Cooking Time:25 Minutes

Ingredients:
- 3 tbsp olive oil
- 1 onion, chopped
- 1 can tomato paste
- ¼ cup red wine vinegar
- 8 fresh sage leaves, chopped
- 2 garlic cloves, minced
- ½ cup water
- 2 cans borlotti beans

Directions:

1. Warm the olive oil in a saucepan over medium heat. Sauté the onion and garlic for 5 minutes, stirring frequently. Add the tomato paste, vinegar, and 1 cup of water, and mix well. Turn the heat to low. Drain and rinse one can of the beans in a colander and add to the saucepan. Pour the entire second can of beans (including the liquid) into the saucepan. Simmer for 10 minutes, stirring occasionally. Serve warm sprinkled with sage.

Nutrition:
- Info Per Serving: Calories: 434;Fat: 2g;Protein: 26g;-Carbs: 80g.

Fruits, Desserts And Snacks

Fruits, Desserts And Snacks

Mini Cucumber & Cream Cheese Sandwiches

Servings:4 | Cooking Time:5 Minutes

Ingredients:
- 4 bread slices
- 1 cucumber, sliced
- 2 tbsp cream cheese, soft
- 1 tbsp chives, chopped
- ¼ cup hummus
- Salt and black pepper to taste

Directions:
1. In a bowl, mix hummus, cream cheese, chives, salt, and pepper until well combined. Spread the mixture onto bread slices. Top with cucumber and cut each sandwich into three pieces. Serve immediately.

Nutrition:
- Info Per Serving: Calories: 190;Fat: 13g;Protein: 9g;-Carbs: 5g.

Pecan & Raspberry & Frozen Yogurt Cups

Servings:4 | Cooking Time:10 Minutes

Ingredients:
- 2 cups fresh raspberries
- 4 cups vanilla frozen yogurt
- 1 lime, zested
- ¼ cup chopped praline pecans

Directions:
1. Divide the frozen yogurt into 4 dessert glasses. Top with raspberries, lime zest, and pecans. Serve immediately.

Nutrition:
- Info Per Serving: Calories: 142;Fat: 3.4g;Protein: 3.7g;-Carbs: 26g.

Chocolate And Avocado Mousse

Servings:4 | Cooking Time: 5 Minutes

Ingredients:
- 8 ounces dark chocolate, chopped
- ¼ cup unsweetened coconut milk
- 2 tablespoons coconut oil
- 2 ripe avocados, deseeded
- ¼ cup raw honey
- Sea salt, to taste

Directions:
1. Put the chocolate in a saucepan. Pour in the coconut milk and add the coconut oil.
2. Cook for 3 minutes or until the chocolate and coconut oil melt. Stir constantly.
3. Put the avocado in a food processor, then drizzle with honey and melted chocolate. Pulse to combine until smooth.
4. Pour the mixture in a serving bowl, then sprinkle with salt. Refrigerate to chill for 30 minutes and serve.

Nutrition:
- Info Per Serving: Calories: 654;Fat: 46.8g;Protein: 7.2g;-Carbs: 55.9g.

Berry Sorbet

Servings:4 | Cooking Time:10 Min + Freezing Time

Ingredients:
- 1 tsp lemon juice
- ¼ cup honey
- 1 cup fresh strawberries
- 1 cup fresh raspberries
- 1 cup fresh blueberries

Directions:
1. Bring 1 cup of water to a boil in a pot over high heat. Stir in honey until dissolved. Remove from the heat and mix in berries and lemon juice; let cool.
2. Once cooled, add the mixture to a food processor and pulse until smooth. Transfer to a shallow glass and freeze for 1 hour. Stir with a fork and freeze for 30 more minutes. Repeat a couple of times. Serve in dessert dishes.

Nutrition:
- Info Per Serving: Calories: 115;Fat: 1g;Protein: 1g;-Carbs: 29g.

Lovely Coconut-covered Strawberries

Servings:4 | Cooking Time:15 Min + Cooling Time

Ingredients:
- 1 cup chocolate chips
- ¼ cup coconut flakes
- 1 lb strawberries
- ½ tsp vanilla extract
- ½ tsp ground nutmeg
- ¼ tsp salt

Directions:
1. Melt chocolate chips for 30 seconds. Remove and stir in vanilla, nutmeg, and salt. Let cool for 2-3 minutes. Dip strawberries into the chocolate and then into the coconut flakes. Place on a wax paper-lined cookie sheet and let sit for 30 minutes until the chocolate dries. Serve.

Nutrition:
- Info Per Serving: Calories: 275;Fat: 20g;Protein: 6g;- Carbs: 21g.

Honey & Spice Roasted Almonds

Servings:4 | Cooking Time:15 Minutes

Ingredients:
- 2 tbsp olive oil
- 3 cups almonds
- 1 tbsp curry powder
- ¼ cup honey
- 1 tsp salt

Directions:
1. Preheat oven to 260 °F. Coat almonds with olive oil, curry powder, and salt in a bowl; mix well. Arrange on a lined with aluminum foil sheet and bake for 15 minutes. Remove from the oven and let cool for 10 minutes. Drizzle with honey and let cool at room temperature. Enjoy!

Nutrition:
- Info Per Serving: Calories: 134;Fat: 8g;Protein: 1g;- Carbs: 18g.

Mint Raspberries Panna Cotta

Servings:4 | Cooking Time:15 Min + Chilling Time

Ingredients:
- 2 tbsp warm water
- 2 tsp gelatin powder
- 2 cups heavy cream
- 1 cup raspberries
- 2 tbsp sugar
- 1 tsp vanilla extract
- 4 fresh mint leaves

Directions:
1. Pour 2 tbsp of warm water into a small bowl. Stir in the gelatin to dissolve. Allow the mixture to sit for 10 minutes.

In a large bowl, combine the heavy cream, raspberries, sugar, and vanilla. Blend with an immersion blender until the mixture is smooth and the raspberries are well puréed. Transfer the mixture to a saucepan and heat over medium heat until just below a simmer. Remove from the heat and let cool for 5 minutes. Add in the gelatin mixture, whisking constantly until smooth. Divide the custard between ramekins and refrigerate until set, 4-6 hours. Serve chilled garnished with mint leaves.

Nutrition:
- Info Per Serving: Calories: 431;Fat: 44g;Protein: 4g;- Carbs: 7g.

Salty Spicy Popcorn

Servings:6 | Cooking Time:10 Minutes

Ingredients:
- 3 tbsp olive oil
- ¼ tsp garlic powder
- Salt and black pepper to taste
- ½ tsp dried thyme
- ½ tsp chili powder
- ½ tsp dried oregano
- 12 cups plain popped popcorn

Directions:
1. Warm the olive oil in a large pan over medium heat. Add the garlic powder, black pepper, salt, chili powder, thyme, and stir oregano until fragrant, 1 minute. Place the popcorn in a large bowl and drizzle with the infused oil over. Toss to coat.

Nutrition:
- Info Per Serving: Calories: 183;Fat: 12g;Protein: 3g;- Carbs: 19g.

Orange Mug Cakes

Servings:2 | Cooking Time: 3 Minutes

Ingredients:
- 6 tablespoons flour
- 2 tablespoons sugar
- 1 teaspoon orange zest
- ½ teaspoon baking powder
- Pinch salt
- 1 egg
- 2 tablespoons olive oil
- 2 tablespoons unsweetened almond milk
- 2 tablespoons freshly squeezed orange juice
- ½ teaspoon orange extract
- ½ teaspoon vanilla extract

Directions:
1. Combine the flour, sugar, orange zest, baking powder, and salt in a small bowl.

2. In another bowl, whisk together the egg, olive oil, milk, orange juice, orange extract, and vanilla extract.

3. Add the dry ingredients to the wet ingredients and stir to incorporate. The batter will be thick.

4. Divide the mixture into two small mugs. Microwave each mug separately. The small ones should take about 60 seconds, and one large mug should take about 90 seconds, but microwaves can vary.

5. Cool for 5 minutes before serving.

Nutrition:
• Info Per Serving: Calories: 303;Fat: 16.9g;Protein: 6.0g;-Carbs: 32.5g.

Mascarpone Baked Pears

Servings:2 | Cooking Time: 20 Minutes

Ingredients:
• 2 ripe pears, peeled
• 1 tablespoon plus 2 teaspoons honey, divided
• 1 teaspoon vanilla, divided
• ¼ teaspoon ground coriander
• ¼ teaspoon ginger
• ¼ cup minced walnuts
• ¼ cup mascarpone cheese
• Pinch salt
• Cooking spray

Directions:
1. Preheat the oven to 350ºF. Spray a small baking dish with cooking spray.

2. Slice the pears in half lengthwise. Using a spoon, scoop out the core from each piece. Put the pears, cut side up, in the baking dish.

3. Whisk together 1 tablespoon of honey, ½ teaspoon of vanilla, ginger, and coriander in a small bowl. Pour this mixture evenly over the pear halves.

4. Scatter the walnuts over the pear halves.

5. Bake in the preheated oven for 20 minutes, or until the pears are golden and you're able to pierce them easily with a knife.

6. Meanwhile, combine the mascarpone cheese with the remaining 2 teaspoons of honey, ½ teaspoon of vanilla, and a pinch of salt. Stir to combine well.

7. Divide the mascarpone among the warm pear halves and serve.

Nutrition:
• Info Per Serving: Calories: 308;Fat: 16.0g;Protein: 4.1g;-Carbs: 42.7g.

Spanish-style Pizza With Jamón Serrano

Servings:4 | Cooking Time:90 Minutes

Ingredients:
• For the crust
• 2 tbsp olive oil
• 2 cups flour
• 1 cup lukewarm water
• 1 pinch of sugar
• 1 tsp active dry yeast
• ¾ tsp salt
• For the topping
• 1/3 cup Spanish olives with pimento
• ½ cup tomato sauce
• ½ cup sliced mozzarella
• 4 oz jamon serrano, sliced
• 7 fresh basil leaves

Directions:
1. Sift the flour and salt in a bowl and stir in yeast. Mix lukewarm water, olive oil, and sugar in another bowl. Add the wet mixture to the dry mixture and whisk until you obtain a soft dough. Place the dough on a lightly floured work surface and knead it thoroughly for 4-5 minutes until elastic. Transfer the dough to a greased bowl. Cover with cling film and leave to rise for 50-60 minutes in a warm place until doubled in size. Roll out the dough to a thickness of around 12 inches.

2. Preheat the oven to 400 °F. Line a pizza pan with parchment paper. Spread the tomato sauce on the crust. Arrange the mozzarella slices on the sauce and then the Jamon serrano. Bake for 15 minutes or until the cheese melts. Remove from the oven and top with olives and basil. Slice and serve warm.

Nutrition:
• Info Per Serving: Calories: 160;Fat: 6g;Protein: 22g;-Carbs: 0.5g.

Artichoke & Sun-dried Tomato Pizza

Servings:4 | Cooking Time:80 Minutes

Ingredients:
• 2 tbsp olive oil
• 1 cup canned passata
• 2 cups flour
• 1 pinch of sugar
• 1 tsp active dry yeast
• ¾ tsp salt
• 1 ½ cups artichoke hearts
• ¼ cup grated Asiago cheese
• ½ onion, minced
• 3 garlic cloves, minced
• 1 tbsp dried oregano
• 6 sundried tomatoes, chopped

- ½ tsp red pepper flakes
- 5-6 basil leaves, torn

Directions:

1. Sift the flour and salt in a bowl and stir in yeast. Mix 1 cup of lukewarm water, olive oil, and sugar in another bowl. Add the wet mixture to the dry mixture and whisk until you obtain a soft dough. Place the dough on a lightly floured work surface and knead it thoroughly for 4-5 minutes until elastic. Transfer the dough to a greased bowl. Cover with cling film and leave to rise for 50-60 minutes in a warm place until doubled in size. Roll out the dough to a thickness of around 12 inches.

2. Preheat oven to 400 °F. Warm oil in a saucepan over medium heat and sauté onion and garlic for 3-4 minutes. Mix in tomatoes and oregano and bring to a boil. Decrease the heat and simmer for another 5 minutes. Transfer the pizza crust to a baking sheet. Spread the sauce all over and top with artichoke hearts and sun-dried tomatoes. Scatter the cheese and bake for 15 minutes until golden. Top with red pepper flakes and basil leaves and serve sliced.

Nutrition:
- Info Per Serving: Calories: 254;Fat: 9.5g;Protein: 8g;-Carbs: 34.3g.

Veggie Pizza With Caramelized Onions

Servings:4 | Cooking Time:90 Minutes

Ingredients:
- For the crust
- 2 tbsp olive oil
- 2 cups flour
- 1 cup lukewarm water
- 1 pinch of sugar
- 1 tsp active dry yeast
- ¾ tsp salt
- For the caramelized onion
- 2 tbsp olive oil
- 1 onion, sliced
- 1 tsp sugar
- ½ tsp salt
- For the pizza
- ¼ cup shaved Pecorino Romano cheese
- 2 tbsp olive oil
- ½ cup grated mozzarella
- 1 cup baby spinach
- ¼ cup chopped fresh basil
- ½ red bell pepper, sliced

Directions:

1. Sift the flour and salt in a bowl and stir in yeast. Mix lukewarm water, olive oil, and sugar in another bowl. Add the wet mixture to the dry mixture and whisk until you obtain a soft dough. Place the dough on a lightly floured work surface and knead it thoroughly until elastic. Transfer the

dough to a greased bowl. Cover with cling film and leave to rise for 50-60 minutes in a warm place until doubled in size. Roll out the dough to a thickness of around 12 inches.

2. Warm olive oil in a skillet over medium heat and sauté onion with salt and sugar for 3 minutes. Lower the heat and brown for 20-35 minutes until caramelized. Preheat oven to 390 °F. Transfer the pizza crust to a baking sheet. Drizzle the crust with olive oil and top with onion. Cover with bell pepper and mozzarella. Bake for 10-15 minutes. Serve topped with baby spinach, basil, and Pecorino cheese.

Nutrition:
- Info Per Serving: Calories: 399;Fat: 22.7g;Protein: 8g;-Carbs: 43g.

Tuna, Tomato & Burrata Salad

Servings:4 | Cooking Time:10 Minutes

Ingredients:
- 2 tbsp extra-virgin olive oil
- 2 tbsp canned tuna, flaked
- 4 heirloom tomato slices
- Salt and black pepper to taste
- 4 burrata cheese slices
- 8 fresh basil leaves, sliced
- 1 tbsp balsamic vinegar

Directions:

1. Place the tomatoes on a plate. Top with burrata slices and tuna. Sprinkle with basil. Drizzle with olive oil and balsamic vinegar and serve.

Nutrition:
- Info Per Serving: Calories: 153;Fat: 13g;Protein: 7g;-Carbs: 2g.

Mini Meatball Pizza

Servings:4 | Cooking Time:25 Minutes

Ingredients:
- 1 pizza crust
- 1 ½ cups pizza sauce
- ½ tsp dried oregano
- 8 oz bite-sized meatballs
- 1 cup bell peppers, sliced
- 2 cups mozzarella, shredded

Directions:

1. Preheat oven to 400 °F. Spread the pizza crust evenly with pizza sauce and sprinkle with oregano. Arrange the meatballs on the pizza sauce. Sprinkle with bell peppers and mozzarella cheese. Bake for about 20 minutes or until the crust is golden brown and cheese melts. Serve immediately.

Nutrition:
- Info Per Serving: Calories: 555;Fat: 28g;Protein: 30g;-Carbs: 45g.

White Bean Dip With Pita Wedges

Servings:4 | Cooking Time:25 Minutes

Ingredients:
- ½ cup olive oil
- 1 garlic clove
- 1 can cannellini beans
- 1 lemon, zested and juiced
- Salt to taste
- ½ tsp oregano
- 4 pitas, cut into wedges
- 5 black olives

Directions:
1. Preheat the oven to 350 °F. Arrange the pita wedges on a baking sheet and sprinkle with salt and oregano; drizzle them with some olive oil. Bake for 10-12 minutes until the pita beginning to brown. Place the beans, garlic, lemon juice, lemon zest, and salt and purée, drizzling in as much olive oil as needed until the beans are smooth. Transfer the dip to a bowl and serve the toasted pita bread.

Nutrition:
- Info Per Serving: Calories: 209;Fat: 17g;Protein: 4g;-Carbs: 12g.

Bruschetta With Tomato & Basil

Servings:4 | Cooking Time:20 Minutes

Ingredients:
- 1 ciabatta loaf, halved lengthwise
- 2 tbsp olive oil
- 3 tbsp basil, chopped
- 4 tomatoes, cubed
- 1 shallot, sliced
- 2 garlic cloves, minced
- Salt and black pepper to taste
- 1 tbsp balsamic vinegar
- ½ tsp garlic powder

Directions:
1. Preheat the oven to 380 °F. Line a baking sheet with parchment paper. Cut in half each half of the ciabatta loaf. Place them on the sheet and sprinkle with some olive oil. Bake for 10 minutes. Mix tomatoes, shallot, basil, garlic, salt, pepper, olive oil, vinegar, and garlic powder in a bowl and let sit for 10 minutes. Apportion the mixture among bread pieces.

Nutrition:
- Info Per Serving: Calories: 170;Fat: 5g;Protein: 5g;-Carbs: 30g.

Portuguese Orange Mug Cake

Servings:2 | Cooking Time:12 Minutes

Ingredients:
- 2 tbsp butter, melted
- 6 tbsp flour
- 2 tbsp sugar
- ½ tsp baking powder
- ¼ tsp salt
- 1 tsp orange zest
- 1 egg
- 2 tbsp orange juice
- 2 tbsp milk
- ½ tsp orange extract
- ½ tsp vanilla extract
- Orange slices for garnish

Directions:
1. In a bowl, beat the egg, butter, orange juice, milk, orange extract, and vanilla extract. In another bowl, combine the flour, sugar, baking powder, salt, and orange zest. Pour the dry ingredients into the wet ingredients and stir to combine. Spoon the mixture into 2 mugs and microwave one at a time for 1-2 minutes. Garnish with orange slices.

Nutrition:
- Info Per Serving: Calories: 302;Fat: 17g;Protein: 6g;-Carbs: 33g.

Eggplant & Pepper Spread On Toasts

Servings:4 | Cooking Time:10 Minutes

Ingredients:
- 1 red bell pepper, roasted and chopped
- 1 lb eggplants, baked, peeled and chopped
- ¾ cup olive oil
- 1 lemon, zested
- 1 red chili pepper, chopped
- 1 ½ tsp capers
- 1 garlic clove, minced
- Salt and black pepper to taste
- 1 baguette, sliced and toasted

Directions:
1. In a food processor, place the eggplants, lemon zest, red chili pepper, bell pepper, garlic, salt, and pepper. Blend while gradually adding the olive oil until smooth. Spread each baguette slice with the spread and top with capers to serve.

Nutrition:
- Info Per Serving: Calories: 364;Fat: 38g;Protein: 1.5g;-Carbs: 9.3g.

Crispy Kale Chips

Servings:4 | Cooking Time:15 Minutes

Ingredients:
- 2 tbsp olive oil
- 2 heads curly leaf kale
- Sea salt to taste

Directions:
1. Tear the kale into bite-sized pieces. Toss with the olive oil, and lay on a baking sheet in a single layer. Sprinkle with a pinch of sea salt. Bake for 10 to 15 minutes until crispy. Serve or store in an airtight container.

Nutrition:
- Info Per Serving: Calories: 102;Fat: 4g;Protein: 6g;-Carbs: 14g.

Stuffed Cucumber Bites

Servings:4 | Cooking Time:10 Minutes

Ingredients:
- ¼ cup extra-virgin olive oil
- 2 cucumbers
- Salt to taste
- 6 basil leaves, chopped
- 1 tbsp fresh mint, minced
- 1 garlic clove, minced
- ¼ cup walnuts, ground
- ¼ cup feta cheese, crumbled
- ½ tsp paprika

Directions:
1. Cut cucumbers lengthwise. With a spoon, remove the seeds and hollow out a shallow trough in each piece. Lightly salt each piece and set aside on a platter. In a bowl, combine the basil, mint, garlic, walnuts, feta, and olive oil and blend until smooth. Spoon the mixture into each cucumber half and sprinkle with paprika. Cut each half into 4 pieces. Serve.

Nutrition:
- Info Per Serving: Calories: 176;Fat: 3g;Protein: 5g;-Carbs: 18g.

Lebanese Spicy Baba Ganoush

Servings:4 | Cooking Time:50 Minutes

Ingredients:
- 2 tbsp olive oil
- 2 eggplants, poked with a fork
- 2 tbsp tahini paste
- 1 tsp cayenne pepper
- 2 tbsp lemon juice
- 2 garlic cloves, minced
- Salt and black pepper to taste
- 1 tbsp parsley, chopped

Directions:
1. Preheat oven to 380 °F. Arrange eggplants on a roasting pan and bake for 40 minutes. Set aside to cool. Peel the cooled eggplants and place them in a blender along with the tahini paste, lemon juice, garlic, cayenne pepper, salt, and pepper. Puree the ingredients while gradually adding olive oil until a smooth and homogeneous consistency. Top with parsley.

Nutrition:
- Info Per Serving: Calories: 130;Fat: 5g;Protein: 5g;-Carbs: 2g.

Garlic-yogurt Dip With Walnuts

Servings:4 | Cooking Time:5 Minutes

Ingredients:
- 2 cups Greek yogurt
- 3 garlic cloves, minced
- ¼ cup dill, chopped
- 1 green onion, chopped
- ¼ cup walnuts, chopped
- Salt and black pepper to taste

Directions:
1. Combine garlic, yogurt, dill, walnuts, salt, and pepper in a bowl. Serve topped with green onion.

Nutrition:
- Info Per Serving: Calories: 210;Fat: 7g;Protein: 9g;-Carbs: 16g.

Crispy Potato Chips

Servings:4 | Cooking Time:40 Minutes

Ingredients:
- 2 tbsp olive oil
- 4 potatoes, cut into wedges
- 2 tbsp grated Parmesan cheese
- Salt and black pepper to taste

Directions:
1. Preheat the oven to 340 °F. In a bowl, combine the potatoes, olive oil, salt, and black pepper. Spread on a lined baking sheet and bake for 40 minutes until the edges are browned. Serve sprinkled with Parmesan cheese.

Nutrition:
- Info Per Serving: Calories: 359;Fat: 8g;Protein: 9g;-Carbs: 66g.

Apples Stuffed With Pecans

Servings:4 | Cooking Time:55 Minutes

Ingredients:
- 2 tbsp brown sugar
- 4 apples, cored
- ¼ cup chopped pecans
- 1 tsp ground cinnamon
- ¼ tsp ground nutmeg
- ¼ tsp ground ginger

Directions:
1. Preheat oven to 375 °F. Arrange the apples cut-side up on a baking dish. Combine pecans, ginger, cinnamon, brown sugar, and nutmeg in a bowl. Scoop the mixture into the apples and bake for 35-40 minutes until golden brown.

Nutrition:
- Info Per Serving: Calories: 142;Fat: 1.1g;Protein: 0.8g;-Carbs: 36g.

Roasted Carrot Ribbons With Mayo Sauce

Servings:4 | Cooking Time:50 Minutes

Ingredients:
- 2 tbsp olive oil
- 1 lb carrots, shaved into ribbons
- Salt and black pepper to taste
- ½ lemon, zested
- 1/3 cup light mayonnaise
- 1 garlic clove, minced
- 1 tsp cumin, ground
- 1 tbsp dill, chopped

Directions:
1. Preheat the oven to 380 °F. Spread carrot ribbons on a paper-lined roasting tray. Drizzle with some olive oil and sprinkle with cumin, salt, and pepper. Roast for 20-25 minutes until crisp and golden. In a bowl, mix mayonnaise, lemon zest, garlic, dill, and remaining olive oil. Serve the roasted carrots with mayo sauce.

Nutrition:
- Info Per Serving: Calories: 200;Fat: 6g;Protein: 6g;-Carbs: 8g.

Salmon-cucumber Rolls

Servings:4 | Cooking Time:5 Minutes

Ingredients:
- 8 Kalamata olives, chopped
- 4 oz smoked salmon strips
- 1 cucumber, sliced lengthwise
- 2 tsp lime juice
- 4 oz cream cheese, soft
- 1 tsp lemon zest, grated
- Salt and black pepper to taste
- 2 tsp dill, chopped

Directions:
1. Place cucumber slices on a flat surface and top each with a salmon strip. Combine olives, lime juice, cream cheese, lemon zest, salt, pepper, and dill in a bowl. Smear cream mixture over salmon and roll them up. Serve immediately.

Nutrition:
- Info Per Serving: Calories: 250;Fat: 16g;Protein: 18g;-Carbs: 17g.

Pesto Arugula Dip

Servings:4 | Cooking Time:5 Minutes

Ingredients:
- 1 cup arugula, chopped
- 3 tbsp basil pesto
- 1 cup cream cheese, soft
- Salt and black pepper to taste
- 1 cup heavy cream
- 1 tbsp chives, chopped

Directions:
1. Combine arugula, basil pesto, salt, pepper, and heavy cream in a blender and pulse until smooth. Transfer to a bowl and mix in cream cheese. Serve topped with chives.

Nutrition:
- Info Per Serving: Calories: 240;Fat: 15g;Protein: 6g;-Carbs: 7g.

Strawberry Parfait

Servings:2 | Cooking Time:10 Minutes

Ingredients:
- ¾ cup Greek yogurt
- 1 tbsp cocoa powder
- ¼ cup strawberries, chopped
- 5 drops vanilla stevia

Directions:
1. Combine cocoa powder, strawberries, yogurt, and stevia in a bowl. Serve immediately.

Nutrition:
- Info Per Serving: Calories: 210;Fat: 9g;Protein: 5g;-Carbs: 8g.

Baby Artichoke Antipasto

Servings:4 | Cooking Time:5 Minutes

Ingredients:
- 1 jar roasted red peppers
- 8 canned artichoke hearts
- 1 can garbanzo beans
- 1 cup whole Kalamata olives
- ¼ cup balsamic vinegar
- Salt to taste
- 1 lemon, zested

Directions:
1. Slice the peppers and put them into a large bowl. Cut the artichoke hearts into quarters, and add them to the bowl. Add the garbanzo beans, olives, balsamic vinegar, lemon zest, and salt. Toss all the ingredients together. Serve chilled.

Nutrition:
- Info Per Serving: Calories: 281;Fat: 15g;Protein: 7g;-Carbs: 30g.

Fancy Baileys Ice Coffee

Servings:4 | Cooking Time:5 Min + Chilling Time

Ingredients:
- 1 cup espresso
- 2 cups milk
- 4 tbsp Baileys
- ½ tsp ground cinnamon
- ½ tsp vanilla extract
- Ice cubes

Directions:
1. Fill four glasses with ice cubes. Mix milk, cinnamon, and vanilla in a food processor until nice and frothy. Pour into the glasses. Combine the Baileys with the espresso and mix well. Pour ¼ of the espresso mixture over the milk and serve.

Nutrition:
- Info Per Serving: Calories: 100;Fat: 5g;Protein: 4g;-Carbs: 8g.

Cucumber Noodles With Goat Cheese

Servings:4 | Cooking Time:5 Minutes

Ingredients:
- ½ cup olive oil
- 2 cucumbers, spiralized
- ½ cup black olives, sliced
- 12 cherry tomatoes, halved
- Salt and black pepper to taste
- 1 small red onion, chopped
- ½ cup goat cheese, crumbled
- ¼ cup apple cider vinegar

Directions:
1. Combine olives, tomatoes, salt, pepper, onion, goat cheese, olive oil, and vinegar in a bowl and mix well. Place the cucumbers on a platter and top with the cheese mixture.

Nutrition:
- Info Per Serving: Calories: 150;Fat: 15g;Protein: 2g;-Carbs: 4g.

Festive Pumpkin Cheesecake

Servings:6 | Cooking Time:50 Min + Chilling Time

Ingredients:
- ½ cup butter, melted
- 1 cup flour
- 1 can pumpkin purée
- 1 ½ cups mascarpone cheese
- ½ cup sugar
- 4 large eggs
- 2 tsp vanilla extract
- 2 tsp pumpkin pie spice

Directions:
1. Preheat oven to 350 °F. In a small bowl, combine the flour and melted butter with a fork until well combined. Press the mixture into the bottom of a greased baking pan. In a large bowl, beat together the pumpkin purée, mascarpone cheese, and sugar using an electric mixer.
2. Add the eggs, one at a time, beating after each addition. Stir in the vanilla and pumpkin pie spice until just combined. Pour the mixture over the crust and bake until set, 40-45 minutes. Allow to cool to room temperature. Refrigerate for at least 6 hours before serving. Serve chilled.

Nutrition:
- Info Per Serving: Calories: 242;Fat: 22g;Protein: 7g;-Carbs: 5g.

Chili & Lemon Shrimp

Servings:6 | Cooking Time:10 Minutes

Ingredients:
- 24 large shrimp, peeled and deveined
- ½ cup olive oil
- 5 garlic cloves, minced
- 1 tsp red pepper flakes
- 1 lemon, juiced and zested
- 1 tsp dried dill
- 1 tsp dried thyme
- Salt and black pepper to taste

Directions:
1. Warm the olive oil in a large skillet over medium heat. Add the garlic and red pepper flakes and cook for 1 minute. Add the shrimp and cook an additional 3 minutes, stirring frequently. Remove from the pan, and sprinkle with lemon

juice, lemon zest, thyme, dill, salt, and pepper. Serve.

Nutrition:
- Info Per Serving: Calories: 198;Fat: 6g;Protein: 9g;-Carbs: 28g.

Mango And Coconut Frozen Pie

Servings:8 | Cooking Time: 0 Minutes

Ingredients:
- Crust:
- 1 cup cashews
- ½ cup rolled oats
- 1 cup soft pitted dates
- Filling:
- 2 large mangoes, peeled and chopped
- ½ cup unsweetened shredded coconut
- 1 cup unsweetened coconut milk
- ½ cup water

Directions:
1. Combine the ingredients for the crust in a food processor. Pulse to combine well.
2. Pour the mixture in an 8-inch springform pan, then press to coat the bottom. Set aside.
3. Combine the ingredients for the filling in the food processor, then pulse to purée until smooth.
4. Pour the filling over the crust, then use a spatula to spread the filling evenly. Put the pan in the freeze for 30 minutes.
5. Remove the pan from the freezer and allow to sit for 15 minutes under room temperature before serving.

Nutrition:
- Info Per Serving: Calories: 426;Fat: 28.2g;Protein: 8.1g;-Carbs: 14.9g.

Grilled Stone Fruit With Honey

Servings:2 | Cooking Time: 6 Minutes

Ingredients:
- 3 apricots, halved and pitted
- 2 plums, halved and pitted
- 2 peaches, halved and pitted
- ½ cup low-fat ricotta cheese
- 2 tablespoons honey
- Cooking spray

Directions:
1. Preheat the grill to medium heat. Spray the grill grates with cooking spray.
2. Arrange the fruit, cut side down, on the grill, and cook for 2 to 3 minutes per side, or until lightly charred and softened.
3. Serve warm with a sprinkle of cheese and a drizzle of honey.

Nutrition:

- Info Per Serving: Calories: 298;Fat: 7.8g;Protein: 11.9g;-Carbs: 45.2g.

Hot Italian Sausage Pizza Wraps

Servings:2 | Cooking Time:20 Minutes

Ingredients:
- 1 tbsp basil, chopped
- 1 tsp olive oil
- 6 oz spicy Italian sausage
- 1 shallot, chopped
- 1 tsp Italian seasoning
- 4 oz marinara sauce
- 2 flour tortillas
- ½ cup mozzarella, shredded
- 1/3 cup Parmesan, grated
- 1 tsp red pepper flakes

Directions:
1. Warm the olive oil in a skillet over medium heat. Add and cook the sausage for 5-6 minutes, stirring and breaking up larger pieces, until cooked through. Remove to a bowl. Sauté the shallot for 3 minutes until soft, stirring frequently. Stir in Italian seasoning, marinara sauce, and reserved sausage. Bring to a simmer and cook for about 2 minutes. Divide the mixture between the tortillas, top with the cheeses, add red pepper flakes and basil, and fold over. Serve immediately.

Nutrition:
- Info Per Serving: Calories: 744;Fat: 46g;Protein: 41g;-Carbs: 40g.

Chocolate, Almond, And Cherry Clusters

Servings:10 | Cooking Time: 3 Minutes

Ingredients:
- 1 cup dark chocolate, chopped
- 1 tablespoon coconut oil
- ½ cup dried cherries
- 1 cup roasted salted almonds

Directions:
1. Line a baking sheet with parchment paper.
2. Melt the chocolate and coconut oil in a saucepan for 3 minutes. Stir constantly.
3. Turn off the heat and mix in the cherries and almonds.
4. Drop the mixture on the baking sheet with a spoon. Place the sheet in the refrigerator and chill for at least 1 hour or until firm.
5. Serve chilled.

Nutrition:
- Info Per Serving: Calories: 197;Fat: 13.2g;Protein: 4.1g;-Carbs: 17.8g.

White Bean Dip The Greek Way

Servings:6 | Cooking Time:5 Minutes

Ingredients:
- ¼ cup extra-virgin olive oil
- 1 lemon, zested and juiced
- 1 can white beans
- 2 garlic cloves, minced
- ¼ tsp ground cumin
- 2 tbsp Greek oregano, chopped
- 1 tsp stone-ground mustard
- Salt to taste

Directions:

1. In a food processor, blend all the ingredients, except for the oregano, until smooth. Top with Greek oregano and serve.

Nutrition:
- Info Per Serving: Calories: 222;Fat: 7g;Protein: 12g;-Carbs: 30.4g.

Hummus & Tomato Stuffed Cucumbers

Servings:2 | Cooking Time:5 Minutes

Ingredients:
- 1 cucumber, halved lengthwise
- ½ cup hummus
- 5 cherry tomatoes, halved
- 2 tbsp fresh basil, minced

Directions:

1. Using a paring knife, scoop most of the seeds from the inside of each cucumber piece to make a cup, being careful not to cut all the way through. Fill each cucumber cup with about 1 tablespoon of hummus. Top with cherry tomatoes and basil.

Nutrition:
- Info Per Serving: Calories: 135;Fat: 6g;Protein: 6g;-Carbs: 16g.

APPENDIX A : 30 Day Meal Plan

	Breakfast	**Lunch**	**Dinner**
Day 1	Spinach Cheese Pie	Saucy Turkey With Ricotta Cheese	Baked Beet & Leek With Dilly Yogurt
Day 2	Sweet Banana Pancakes With Strawberries	Eggplant & Chicken Skillet	Stir-fried Kale With Mushrooms
Day 3	Pecan & Peach Parfait	Herby Turkey Stew	Wilted Dandelion Greens With Sweet Onion
Day 4	Avocado & Tuna Sandwiches	Tunisian Baharaat Grilled Chicken	Garlicky Zucchini Cubes With Mint
Day 5	Carrot & Pecan Cupcakes	Pan-fried Chili Sea Scallops	Baby Kale And Cabbage Salad
Day 6	Tomato Scrambled Eggs With Feta Cheese	Portuguese-style Chicken Breasts	Roasted Asparagus With Hazelnuts
Day 7	Morning Baklava French Toast	Hake Fillet In Herby Tomato Sauce	Tomatoes Filled With Tabbouleh
Day 8	Easy Buckwheat Porridge	Thyme Zucchini & Chicken Stir-fry	Tomatoes Filled With Tabbouleh 111
Day 9	Brown Rice And Black Bean Burgers	Bell Pepper & Scallop Skillet	Baked Vegetable Stew
Day 10	Vegetable & Egg Sandwiches	Spinach Chicken With Chickpeas	Spicy Potato Wedges
Day 11	Chickpea Lettuce Wraps	Crispy Herb Crusted Halibut	Minty Broccoli & Walnuts
Day 12	Hot Egg Scramble	Chicken Cacciatore	Spicy Kale With Almonds
Day 13	Falafel Balls With Tahini Sauce	Lemon Rosemary Roasted Branzino	Homemade Vegetarian Moussaka
Day 14	Grilled Caesar Salad Sandwiches	Zesty Turkey Breast	Sweet Potato Chickpea Buddha Bowl
Day 15	Tomato & Prosciutto Sandwiches	Tuna Gyros With Tzatziki	Ratatouille

	Breakfast	**Lunch**	**Dinner**
Day 16	Parsley Tomato Eggs	Tasty Chicken Pot	Hot Turnip Chickpeas
Day 17	Garlic Bell Pepper Omelet	Lemony Shrimp With Orzo Salad	Stuffed Portobello Mushroom With Tomatoes
Day 18	Fluffy Almond Flour Pancakes With Strawberries	Saucy Green Pea & Chicken	Baked Potato With Veggie Mix
Day 19	Oven-baked Mozzarella Cheese Cups	Seafood Stew	Baked Tomatoes And Chickpeas
Day 20	Cheese & Mushroom Muffins	Simple Chicken With Olive Tapenade	Roasted Vegetable Medley
Day 21	Napoli Scrambled Eggs With Anchovies	Veggie & Clam Stew With Chickpeas	Sautéed Spinach And Leeks
Day 22	Cream Peach Smoothie	Chicken Tagine With Vegetables	Asparagus & Mushroom Farro
Day 23	Power Green Smoothie	Baked Fish With Pistachio Crust	Parmesan Asparagus With Tomatoes
Day 24	Chia & Almond Oatmeal	Chicken Bake With Cottage Cheese	Steamed Beetroot With Nutty Yogurt
Day 25	Basic Tortilla De Patatas	One-skillet Salmon With Olives & Escarole	Grilled Vegetable Skewers
Day 26	Banana & Chocolate Porridge	Hot Tomato & Caper Squid Stew	Sweet Mustard Cabbage Hash
Day 27	Spicy Tofu Tacos With Cherry Tomato Salsa	Roman-style Cod	Cauliflower Cakes With Goat Cheese
Day 28	Baked Honey Acorn Squash	Lemon Trout With Roasted Beets	Simple Braised Carrots
Day 29	Stir-fry Baby Bok Choy	Lemon Grilled Shrimp	Vegetable And Tofu Scramble
Day 30	Maple Peach Smoothie	Trout Fillets With Horseradish Sauce	Cauliflower Hash With Carrots

APPENDIX B: Recipes Index

Bread
Morning Baklava French Toast 3
Vegetable & Egg Sandwiches 5

Broccoli
Minty Broccoli & Walnuts 42
Roasted Vegetable Medley 46
Garlicky Broccoli Rabe 51
Cheese & Broccoli Quiche 53
Simple Green Rice 66
Pesto Fusilli With Broccoli 67
Brussels Sprout
Brussels Sprouts Linguine 49
One-pot Linguine With Brussels Sprouts 75

C

Cabbage
Sweet Mustard Cabbage Hash 49
Baby Kale And Cabbage Salad 41

Carrot
Carrot & Pecan Cupcakes 3
Simple Braised Carrots 50
Roasted Carrot Ribbons With Mayo Sauce 85
Carrot & Barley Risotto 71
Moroccan-Style Vegetable Bean Stew 70

Cauliflower
Paprika Cauliflower Steaks With Walnut Sauce 45
Cauliflower Cakes With Goat Cheese 50
Cauliflower Hash With Carrots 51

Cheese
Rigatoni With Peppers & Mozzarella 72
Italian Tarragon Buckwheat 73

Cherry Tomato
Napoli Scrambled Eggs With Anchovies 9
Lemon Rosemary Roasted Branzino 29
Baked Tomatoes And Chickpeas 46
Parmesan Asparagus With Tomatoes 48
Bell Pepper & Chickpea Salad 59
Hummus & Tomato Stuffed Cucumbers 88

Chicken
Tzatziki Chicken Loaf 19
Chicken Meatballs With Peach Topping 22
Milanese-Style Risotto 66

Chicken Breast
Balsamic Chicken Breasts With Feta 15
Eggplant & Chicken Skillet 16
Tunisian Baharaat Grilled Chicken 16
Portuguese-style Chicken Breasts 17
Thyme Zucchini & Chicken Stir-fry 18
Spinach Chicken With Chickpeas 18
Spinach-Ricotta Chicken Rolls 18
Saucy Green Pea & Chicken 22
Greek Wraps 23
Simple Chicken With Olive Tapenade 24
Chicken Bake With Cottage Cheese 25
Creamy Saffron Chicken With Ziti 65
Chicken Linguine A La Toscana 73

Chicken Thighs
Chicken Cacciatore 20
Tasty Chicken Pot 20
Chicken Tagine With Vegetables 25

Chicken Wing
Italian-style Chicken Stew 56

Chickpea
Chickpea Lettuce Wraps 5
Falafel Balls With Tahini Sauce 6

Classic Socca 13
Veggie & Clam Stew With Chickpeas 30
Sweet Potato Chickpea Buddha Bowl 43
Hot Turnip Chickpeas 44
Israeli Style Eggplant And Chickpea Salad 68
Classic Falafel 71

Chocolate
Chocolate And Avocado Mousse 79
Chocolate, Almond, And Cherry Clusters 87

Chorizo
Kale & Bean Soup With Chorizo 57

Cod Fillet
Roman-Style Cod 32
Cod Fettuccine 33

Couscous
Apricot & Almond Couscous 68

K

Kale
Stir-fried Kale With Mushrooms 40
Spicy Kale With Almonds 42
Sautéed Kale With Olives 63
Crispy Kale Chips 84

L

Lamb
Greek-Style Lamb Burgers 17
Date Lamb Tangine 18
Slow Cook Lamb Shanks With Cannellini Beans Stew 21
Citrusy Leg Lamb 21

M

Mango
Mango And Coconut Frozen Pie 87

Mushroom
Cheese & Mushroom Muffins 9
Stuffed Portobello Mushroom With Tomatoes 45
Baked Potato With Veggie Mix 45
Simple Mushroom Barley Soup 60
Leftover Pasta & Mushroom Frittata 75

O

Oat
Chia & Almond Oatmeal 11

Onion
Wilted Dandelion Greens With Sweet Onion 40
Stir-fry Baby Bok Choy 43
Veggie Pizza With Caramelized Onions 82

Orange
Orange Mug Cakes 80
Portuguese Orange Mug Cake 83

P

Pancetta
Pancetta-wrapped Scallops 35

Pea
Barley, Parsley, And Pea Salad 60
Black-eyed Pea And Vegetable Stew 65

Peach
Maple Peach Smoothie 8
Grilled Stone Fruit With Honey 87

Pear
Greens, Fennel, And Pear Soup With Cashews 55
Mascarpone Baked Pears 81

Penne Pasta
Cilantro Turkey Penne With Asparagus 17

Plain Yogurt
Herby Yogurt Sauce 54

Pork
Tender Pork Shoulder 16
Rich Pork In Cilantro Sauce 21
Sweet Pork Stew 21
Milky Pork Stew 23
Tuscan Pork Cassoulet 23
Chili Pork Rice 76

Pork Chop
Crispy Pork Chops 24
Pork & Mushroom Stew 58

Pork Loin Chop
Pork Chops In Tomato Olive Sauce 15
Baked Garlicky Pork Chops 22

Pork Tenderloin
Spinach-Cheese Stuffed Pork Loin 17
Pork Tenderloin With Caraway Seeds 24

Potato
Basic Tortilla De Patatas 12
Spicy Potato Wedges 42
Zesty Spanish Potato Salad 54
Egg & Potato Salad 56
Parmesan Roasted Red Potatoes 58
Swoodles With Almond Butter Sauce 69
Crispy Potato Chips 84

Prosciutto
Tomato & Prosciutto Sandwiches 7

70968945R00064